I0107545

MY GYPSY LIFE

A ROAD TO HAPPINESS

A MEMOIR

MY GYPSY LIFE

A ROAD TO HAPPINESS

By Rhona Villanueva

Copyright © 2015 by Rhona Villanueva.
All rights reserved.
Available from Amazon
ISBN-10: 0692538283
ISBN-13:978-0692538289

EUROPE

Trinidad and Tobago
Venezuela
Guyana
French Guiana
Colombia
Ecuador
Suriname
Peru
Brazil
Bolivia
South Pacific Ocean
Paraguay
Chile
Argentina
Uruguay
South Atlantic Ocean
Falkland Islands

SOUTH AMERICA

For my children
Anabelle and Alan
and my grandchildren
Austin, Carson
and Leyton
with all my love

INDEX

INTRODUCTION

ESTONIA
    A SLEIGH RIDE   1
    MY MOM   5
    MY DAD   15

GERMANY
    FIREWORK   35
    A LONG JOURNEY SEEKING SAFETY   39
    HOHENFELD 1945   51
    HOHENFELD 1946-1949   57
    CHANGE OF HEMISPHERES   65
    CROSSING THE ATLANTIC   73

CHILE
    A NEW BEGINNING   79
    INDEPENDENCE   83
    MY LAST SCHOOL YEARS   87
    A TRIP TO LLIFEN   95
    SANTA JUANA   99
    A DAY IN THE COUNTRY   103
    EL LLAIMA   107
    THE GYPSY BARON   113
    COLORED MARBLES   117
    DECISIONS   121
    MALLOCO   125
    SCOOTERS ANSD CARS   133
    GREAT SHAKE   137
    TRAVEL PLANS   141

UNITED STATES

    SEPTEMBER 1961   149

    A NEW START IN LONG BEACH   157

    XIMENO   165

    OUR FIRST HOUSE ON ROSE STREET   173

    ON THE MOVE AGAIN   181

    FOUNTAIN VALLEY   185

    VISITING ESTONIA   195

APPENDIX

    ESTONIA   221

    PATERNAL ANCESTORS   225

    OSCAR WILHELM BRASCHE   235

    MATERNAL ANCESTORS   239

    MY GRANDMOTHER MENSENKAMPFF   251

    MY UNCLE CURT VON MENSENKAMPFF   261

    AUNT RITA VON SCHULMANN   275

INTRODUCTION

We Baltic Germans are a group of people that lived in Estonia, Latvia and Lithuania for about seven hundred years. It was our home built through hard work, sacrifice and endurance. Through all those years we maintained our German heritage and the German language.

Then in 1939 political circumstances forced us to leave our homes. A Russian invasion was imminent and nobody wanted to live under Soviet rule. Leaving all our worldly possessions behind, we had to start all over again, grow new roots and find new means of earning a living.

We returned to Germany, the country we had originally come from, and there we endured WW II. After the war ended in 1945, a great many Baltic Germans emigrated to Canada and the United States, others to South America, Australia and England. Families were spread far apart.

The next generation adopted the new country as their home. They learned only through lively nostalgic conversations among parents and relatives, and old pictures what Baltic ways used to be. With the fall of the "Iron Curtain", they and their children now have the opportunity to visit the free Baltic States. Many are driven by curiosity to see what the land of their forefathers is like even though much has changed.

Knowledge of what was has dwindled with the passing of the first generation that left. Family history becomes forgotten. Not enough has been written down for others to read, learn and enjoy. For Baltic Germans, life in the Baltic countries is a chapter in history that has come to an end.

I was born in Tallinn, Estonia, on June 13, 1934, but have no recollection of my early years there. What I do remember about Estonia from conversations between my parents, relatives and friends, and memories from WW II and the years thereafter, I put on paper as best as I could. Maybe in future years some of my descendants will be curious enough to read what happened so many years ago.

Rhona Villanueva

October 1, 2015

A SLEIGH RIDE

Feverishly, my paternal grandparents Arvid and Alma Brasche packed much needed food and warm clothing for themselves and their five children. At midnight the pastor of a neighboring village came with two sleighs. It was pitch-dark. Clouds covered the moon. Quickly and without much talk the sleighs were loaded.

"You have to be very, very quiet now, no talking at all or just in whispers. It is very important for you to remember this," my grandfather told his kids in a low voice before leaving the house.

The children, bundled in thick fur blankets, were distributed in the two sleighs. The friendly pastor, his trustworthy helper and the three oldest children, Dieter (13), Brigitte (11) and Ulrich, my dad (9), were in the first sleigh and my grandparents with the two younger ones, Juergen (6) and Arvid (5), in the second. Off they went into the night on silent runners.

They used only the safer back roads. The main streets were full of Russian military retreating to their homeland and capable of horrendous cruelties. Nobody spoke, all were tense, and their thoughts were racing. Just a few commands to the horses could be heard, along with the soft noises made by their leather harnesses, and the crunching sound of frozen snow breaking up under the weight of the sleighs.

Earlier that day the pastor had come over to talk to my grandfather, also a pastor. He had a somber expression on his face and they talked in a low and secretive voice, making sure that nobody was around to overhear their conversation.

"I found out that the Russians are leaving tomorrow, retreating toward the East."

"Oh, is that from a reliable source?"

"Yes, very reliable, and I was also told that the orders are not to leave any Baltic Germans behind alive."

They both knew that these were not empty threats. Immediately the decision was made to leave that same night toward the coast and the German troops. The pastor promised to come at midnight with two sleighs. My grandfather gratefully accepted this offer since he could not use his own horses and sleighs because the coachman was "Red" (a Bolshevik) and would have alerted the Russians.

What a gift to have trustful and dependable friends in times of need!

It was mid-February of the year 1918, the last year of World War I. The winter had come with all its force. Temperatures were in the teens and daylight was short. Russian soldiers were all over the northern part of Estonia, and farmers were forced to put them up in their houses and barns. Baltic Germans were treated as enemies, even though they all were Russian subjects. Within minutes half of my grandfather's home had to be evacuated. Straw was put on the nice wooden floors to sleep on and about 100 Russians moved in.

And now my grandpa and his family were in their sleighs hoping to get safely and undetected to their destination, the rapidly advancing German front. After a couple of hours, my grandfather took the lead with his sleigh, since the pastor was not familiar with the territory anymore. It was out of his parish. They went on for what seemed to be a very long time.

Suddenly my granddad turned into a farm on the side of the road, not knowing who lived there. They were all cold and the horses needed a rest. He approached the house and wanted to knock, when the door opened and a man stood in the doorway.

"Pastor Brasche, is that you? What are you doing here? Come in quick!"

Grandfather was shocked to see this man who had been a member of his congregation some years back. When he moved away, contact was lost.

"Olaf, I can't believe it's you! I didn't know you live here."

They all hurried inside and gathered in the large and warm kitchen.

"We are on the way to the island Muhu, the German front. The situation is not safe at home. We have one hundred Russians in our house."

"It's not good here either. You were lucky to pick our house. Had you gone to the house before or the farm further down, you would have fallen into the hands of the 'Reds'. How can we help you? What do you need?"

"We just need to rest the horses for a while and the kids are cold and need to go potty. We all could use some hot tea. Do you know the best way to cross the sea to get to Muhu?"

"I will tell Kristian, our son, how to go and he can show you the way."

After what seemed to be a very short rest they continued the journey with the son of those good people as their guide. As it turned out, they were close to the coastline. Now it could get really dangerous. Without the cover of the surrounding woods and underbrush, they could be seen from far away. Besides, there was no protection from the icy wind.

The young lad put on his ice skates and went ahead of them over the frozen sea along the shore. This way, if they got caught, he could get away, pretending not to be part of the group. After a while he told my grandfather which general direction he had to go to reach the next "friendly" farmhouse on a small peninsula. After many "good byes" and "thank yous," he went back and the small group ventured on.

All of a sudden two sleighs were approaching at high speed from the left in their direction. Hearts almost stopped. Granddad kept on going without hesitation. Then everybody realized that those were drunken Russian seamen who were deserting and not interested in them at all. They had their own problems and wanted to get back to Mother Russia.

Shortly before nightfall, they reached their safe haven where they could spend the night. Several other families had made it there before them. Early next morning, the whole group set out over the frozen Baltic Sea toward the island Muhu. The ice was thick. Every so often a loud bang could be heard, like a gunshot fired into the air. It was the ice that cracked and split with the frigid cold. The horses snorted, their breaths visible in the cold air. They were fidgety and scared by the unknown. Instincts took over, but finally they obeyed and went on under the strong guidance of their drivers. This continued for some time.

Finally they saw land in the far distance. Was this it? They hurried on and went up an embankment and out of nowhere came a German voice: "Wer da?" (Who is there?) It was the German outpost on Kesselaid, a tiny uninhabited island before Muhu, and they were safe.

They were told to continue on and cross the ice to Muhu. They let the horses go at a slow pace until they reached the island and a school where many other families had taken refuge as well. A thick layer of straw was on the floors to sleep on and a large kitchen provided the possibility to cook a hot meal.

Their good friend, the pastor, went back with his sleighs. Grandpa followed with the advancing Germans, and in a week's time returned with his own horses and sleighs to take the family home.

This fast advance of the German troops saved many Baltic German lives. Little did they know then that twenty-one years later war would again sweep through Estonia with the start of World War II.

MOM

Mom had a life that should have been perfect in every aspect. She was born into a nice family that was well educated and well to do. Her grandparents travelled extensively abroad. Winters were spent in the big cities. They had a large three-story house, built in the nineteenth century, in the university town of Tartu. The big hall served not only for family gatherings, but was large enough to have lectures there, music performances, interesting discussions or other intellectual functions.

Unfortunately, Mom's generation came too late to enjoy this affluence. Even her parents only experienced the end tail of this comfortable lifestyle which was cut short by the Russian revolution of 1905 and later WW I. These two events had enormous life-changing consequences not only in the Baltic territory but also worldwide.

In 1905 Russia lost the war with Japan. Discontent led to a revolutionary movement that spilled over to the Baltic region. In their frenzy hundreds of manor houses were ransacked, destroyed, and people killed. It was chaos. Then tension subsided somewhat until the begin of WW 1 in 1914.

Mom was born in that small window of calm in Tarvastu, Estonia, on December 4, 1909, and named Karin Gabriele von Mensenkampff. She was the youngest of four children. The two older brothers, Curt and Otto were born in 1902 and 1903, and her sister Rita in 1907.

Her early childhood was a happy one. She and her sister played well together. Many toys were handmade, dogs their constant companions, and the outdoors provided much entertainment. Both girls had long brown hair held together with a colorful bow, only Mom's hair was curlier than her sister's. She also looked more like her mother with soft features and big hazel eyes; whereas Rita resembled her father with his more rectangular face, thin lips and deep-set eyes.

"Mama, please come and tell us a story" was their nightly call to their mother after the nanny had put them to bed. And she came, sat on one of the beds, then the other and they discussed the happy and sad occurrences of the past days.

5

"Now tell us something from when you were little," the girls pleaded, and then their mom reminisced about her own childhood until the girls closed their eyes and fell soundly asleep.

Early on, "Mademoiselle," their live-in governess, spoke to them in French and then home-schooled them. When Mom was about five years old and her sister seven, they were each given a pony, called Mikka and Mokka, which they rode bareback or just with a blanket. The little girls could not be happier. They had grown up around horses and were not afraid of them. They loved them and in later years became excellent riders.

A year later the family decided to move to their house in nearby Viljandi. World War 1 had started. Political unrest again had spread throughout the region and was on the rise. The family felt more protected and secure in that little town. Mom and her sister liked it in Viljandi. It was something different and exciting, so much new to see. It was like moving to a big city, since their birthplace Tarvastu was just a large farm with houses and barns, and extensive fields and forests. The girls were unaware of what was happening in their country and the danger everybody was in. They just considered it a nice change.

The move was necessary for another reason as well: their home in Tarvastu had been requisitioned by the Russians and converted into a hospital for their wounded soldiers. Her father was forced to agree to this in order to avoid deportation to Siberia and death. Not long after, the wooden house burned to the ground due to the carelessness of the soldiers. The hospital then was moved to another large home where their grandparents had lived before taking refuge in Viljandi. The manor house had already been destroyed by the Russians in 1905 when they ransacked the country and burned hundreds of houses.

The unstable political and economical situation, as well as the ongoing war, brought forth another life-changing decision in 1918. The women should go to Germany to escape harm in their homeland. Mom, her sister Rita, their mother and their grandmother Ungern-Sternberg were to leave for Riga, Latvia, and then book passages on a ship with destination Germany. A young Estonian servant came with them to assist their mother who was not well and walked with the help of canes due to MS. Mom's two brothers would remain with their father.

This move was not very well accepted by the girls Rita and Karin. A train ride was maybe interesting, but they had to leave their beloved ponies behind. And why did they have to move again? They were happy in Viljandi.

"Girls, just think how interesting it will be traveling to Germany. In Riga we will board a big ship that takes us to a German port and from there we will travel by train. You will have a lot of fun. You will see so many new things," their mother told them. "Your dad will take care of Mikka and Mokka. They will be fine." She explained to them the facts of war, that it was not safe any longer to stay in Estonia. Mom and Rita had seen many German soldiers in Viljandi, even officers in their own home, had heard shooting, and they then realized and accepted the fact that it would be better to leave.

The little group arrived in Riga. The city was full of German soldiers. There were no Russians in sight. They felt secure, and when their mother was assured by a German commander that the army would be there for a long time, she decided to stay in Riga, thinking the worst was over.

It proved to be a big mistake.

After several weeks, upon orders from the German Reich, the military left within a few days. The same German commander sent a note to her mother warning her about the retreat, but it was too late to secure passage on a ship or find seats on a train. The family was trapped.

The city of Riga was occupied by hordes of Bolsheviks and revolutionary elements, and the family had to endure the worst hardships imaginable. Persecutions of Germans and especially of German aristocrats was rampant. Arrests were on the daily agenda. Prisons were filled to capacity.

People stayed in their homes and hid behind closed doors and windows. Many stores closed for lack of merchandise. Suppliers were scared and avoided the city. Food became scarce. Family and friends helped each other and shared whatever they had. Children were safer on the streets than adults; therefore, Mom and her sister were sent to known remaining stores to trade their mother's jewelry for anything edible they could get. Cash was not wanted.

Besides feeding themselves, people also had to take care of their loved ones in prison. Prisoners received only one slice of stale bread each day and a bucket of water to be shared by all, but only if they were lucky and somebody remembered to hand it out. In many ways conditions could be compared to Medieval times. There were thirty or forty people in badly lit ice-cold rooms with poor ventilation, with barely enough space to lie down on the hard floor, side by side, touching each other. Ironically people often welcomed these tight quarters just to keep warm.

When rumors surfaced that an army of Latvian and German volunteers was forming, hope spread among the population of Riga. Maybe there was an end in sight to this suffering. Maybe, just maybe they could beat the Russians, even thought they were outnumbered ten to one.

Summer turned into winter and the city began to freeze. The daily executions of prisoners began. The guards read the names from a list, one by one, and then led them outside. Russian soldiers walked them in a single file through heavy snow to their final destination, from where nobody returned.

After many weeks of misery, an army of Latvian and Baltic German volunteers entered the city and liberated Riga from the Bolsheviks but for many, men and women alike, it was too late.

Having this small window of freedom, the family was able to leave and travel to Dresden, Germany, where their grandmother had bought a large villa they all could live in. Fortunately, there were many other Baltic Germans in Dresden who visited each other frequently and helped out as needed.

Mom and Rita were enrolled in school and life began to take a more normal course for them. A year later, in 1920, Mom's brother Curt joined them there with the intention of starting his studies at the university. Mom's other brother Otto remained in Estonia with his father.

"Mom, were you crying? What is the matter? Why are you so sad?" the girls asked their mother anxiously one day upon returning from school. They noticed sad faces all around them. What had happened? And then they were told that back home in Estonia their brother Otto had succumbed to meningitis. He was not quite 20 years old. This was a very sad day for everybody and many tears were shed!

The year 1924, was not a good year either. Their grandmother sold the house and returned to Estonia, forcing them to move to an apartment. Mom's parents divorced and her mother was alone now with the two girls and their brother, Curt. Luckily, financially they could make ends meet spending money wisely. Before Mom's grandfather, Oswald von Ungern-Sternberg, died in 1907, he had deposited some money in a German bank in her mother's name. Had he foreseen the events to come? Was he worried about his ailing daughter?

When her brother Curt finished his studies, Germany was hit by a great depression. Unemployment was high and he could not find a job, more so, since he was considered a foreigner from Estonia. When in 1927 an opportunity presented itself to move to Chile, South America, he took the chance and left. It was a hard decision for him, as well as for his mother. She had to let him go, knowing that she probably would not see him again. They all missed him terribly, most of all her mother.

"Girls, we will return to Estonia," my grandmother told her daughters Karin and Rita shortly after her son had left. "We have been here long enough, going on nine years. We can't stay here forever. It is time to go. I am homesick and very tired." And so they left to return to their homeland.

It was not an easy trip. Mom's mother was confined to a wheelchair by now, had lost her eyesight, and needed constant help. After arriving in Viljandi they tried to adapt to their new surroundings. In the nine years of absence much had changed. The war had ended and the new Estonian Republic was born with all its new rules and regulations. For Mom and her sister everything was new since they had left at a young age.

"Let's go outside, Mama. It is a very pleasant day without wind. It will do us good to breathe some fresh air," Mom told her mother as she pushed the wheelchair towards the door. Her mother was happy to be outside. All the different country smells brought back memories, especially those of her beloved horses. In her younger years, before the illness disabled her, she was a passionate rider. This gift she passed on to her daughters, especially Rita. Now she could not ride anymore, but just touching their baby-soft muzzles and hearing their snorts made her feel better. Mom took her on daily outings, which they both enjoyed.

After approximately one year, Rita moved away to study medicine. Mom, the only child left at home, took care of her mother, but also had fun with friends. She was turning into a beautiful young lady. Her brown wavy hair was cut short now. She had a well proportioned oval face with a clear complexion, full lips, and big hazel eyes. Her nicely shaped body was always slender.

In time she had several suitors, but she was not interested in marriage as yet. She did not want to follow in her sister's footsteps. She had married at twenty years of age, given up her studies in medicine, and was divorced three years later.

Then in 1932 my mother met Ulrich Brasche at her uncle's garage. She had heard of him before from her grandmother but never made his acquaintance. Mom liked his sense of humor. He was courteous and had good manners. His blue eyes were intensely focused and she knew him to be intelligent. He was slender, her same age, and well known in Estonia through his flying. He made a big impression on her, and she changed her mind about marriage. Soon after, they got engaged and married six months later.

They moved to a house in Viljandi, in walking distance from her mother's place. It had a big orchard and garden. There was a barn for poultry and some pigs. A well was in the center of the yard and the barn was large enough to also serve as a garage, first for their BMW motorcycle with a side car, and later their Ford.

They were happy and thought life was wonderful.

Dad became busy working in the garage of Heinz v. Ungern-Sternberg, Mom's uncle, building gliders and flying them, and teaching others how to do the same. He also flew a lot in his small single-engine plane. At times he delivered mail to the islands, took busy merchants to their meetings, or simply flew with Mom for the fun of it.

The liberation movement in Estonia also kept him busy with flights to different parts of the small country. The movement was a power struggle between two political parties. One, headed by Konstantin Päts, suspected to be on Russian payroll, which was confirmed years later, and the other by Arthur Sirk, who wanted to free Estonia from corruption and mismanagement.

On June 13, 1934, I was born to make the family complete. They enjoyed the next five months with a new baby. It was summer, the weather warm. They went boating on a nearby lake and friends and family came for visits.

Then disaster struck.

On November 11, 1934, Dad and Heinz were incarcerated, accused of helping Arthur Sirk, leader of the liberation movement, escape from prison and flying him to Helsinki, Finland. And bad luck continued. Within a three weeks time Mom lost her mother, her grandmother and her grandmother-in-law.

One blow after another had come Mom's way. It was hard for her to lose these loved ones in such a short time. On top of that, she was alone, not knowing what was going to happen to her husband. Political investigations were always dangerous. Facts could be distorted or not presented at all, depending on the investigators. Political interests of the accuser played a role and verdicts could be bought. Anything was possible. One just had to wait, as hard as it was.

Christmas and New Year's-day came and went. Snow covered the landscape. It seemed like life had come to a standstill. It was freezing cold. Mom imagined her husband in that cold cell all by himself. She wept, hidden in her room holding her baby.

Karin, Rita, Otto, Curt and dad Karl von Mensenkampff

Mom's birthplace Tarvastu

Mom with her brother Curt

Karin (l) and Rita (r) on their horses

My mom Karin von Mensenkampff

MY DAD

"You have a boy. Looks to be a healthy one too," the midwife said to my grandfather through the half-open door. He had been anxiously waiting in his office in the back of the house hoping for good news. He was thinking about his children. So far only two babies out of four had survived. Would this newborn grow up to become an adult or join the two little baby sisters in the cemetery who didn't make it past four months of age? The news made him happier than he had been in a long time. Maybe God had listened to his daily prayers.

The boy was baptized Ulrich but called Uli, and he was my dad.

He was a healthy and happy boy, mischievous, too, at times. When punished he had to sit in a corner of a room facing the wall. That did not last long because for entertainment he picked off the wallpaper which got him into more trouble. He had blond hair, blue eyes and grew up fluent in Estonian and German, as had many generations before. It was a strict rule at home to speak German with parents, siblings and the countless relatives.

At the beginning he and his older brother and sister were schooled at home for lack of a German school close by. It was a widespread custom then to have a live-in tutor for a few years. They were mostly graduate students seeking life experience. As the time came to learn more advanced and complicated subjects than reading, writing and arithmetic, the children were sent to live with their mother's brother, uncle Bruno Sellheim. He lived in Viljandi, about 50 miles east of Kullamaa. His house was big enough to accommodate his own family of four children, plus his niece and, eventually, three nephews.

Viljandi was a small town next to a big lake. It had a large Baltic-German population and, therefore, also a German school. On a cliff-like hill overlooking the lake were the ruins of a fort built in the early thirteenth century. This fort, which in the mid-sixteenth century was transformed into a castle, was one of the largest in the Baltic region and a major fortification. At the beginning of the seventeenth century, the castle changed ownership several times and finally fell into ruins. It then became a haven for young boys to explore and make use of their imagination. In later years it was transformed into an outdoor theater.

My dad was a good student when he wanted to be. In chemistry and physics he was the professor's lab assistant. He loved pranks and always found collaborators. When the school acquired a film projector, a new invention, he ran films backwards, to the delight of his fellow students. In chemistry he mixed certain substances producing a terrible stench and, therefore, forcing the teacher to dismiss the class. School vacations brought all the children back home again.

"Did you play your quartz radio again in front of the church? Most folks were late for my sermon" my grandfather, who was the local pastor, said angrily. "Don't do that again."

"But you know, they like to listen to it. It's something new and exiting they have never heard or seen before. It is one of the first radios in Estonia," my dad countered.

He just loved everything mechanical. Old clocks, motors, anything he could disassemble and then put together again fascinated him. As a teenager he drove the tractor during summer vacations working the land belonging to the church. After finishing high school, he stayed on to help his dad with farming. But he did not like it.

He decided to do his obligatory one-year Estonian military service. In 1930 he was denied entrance to the Estonian air force for being *German*, even though he had the Estonian citizenship, was born there as well as his parents and generations before them. He then joined the army and obtained a drivers license for any motorized vehicle, from motorcycles to tanks.

Having served his year with the military, he looked for a job. My grandmother's brother, Heinz von Ungern-Sternberg, recognized his mechanical talents and put him in charge of his garage in Viljandi. Heinz, only nine years older than Dad, was interested in flying and talked my dad into entering a glider pilot school in Rositten. Dad was very excited about this idea and within one month passed all three available courses. The normal time was one month for each course. A new passion had taken hold of him. Flying!

Starting in 1931, he and Heinz attended classes at the Tallinn Aviation Society. In July of 1932 they passed all the required written, oral and flying tests to fly privately and also commercially, which allowed them to transport passengers, baggage and freight. They were the second and third pilots in Estonian history to obtain this license.

Together with Heinz and with his backing, Dad built the first glider in Estonia. They taught others how to build their own and gave lessons to fly them. In March of 1933 Dad bought the remains of a crash-landed Klemm L 25 Hirth with the intention to rebuild it.

Early in 1932, Dad met Karin, Heinz's niece, who lived in Viljandi with her mother. It must have been love at first sight. They were engaged in November 1932 and married in a civil ceremony on May 20, 1933. A new motor for that crashed plane was a wedding present from his mother–in–law, Alexandrine Emily von Mensenkampff, my grandmother.

When I was born a year later in Tallinn, Dad picked us up from the hospital and flew us home to Viljandi. The wrecked airplane was rebuilt by then and in excellent flying condition and so I became the youngest passenger in Estonian history.

The early thirties were difficult years. The worldwide economic crisis had also reached Estonia. The Estonian government was in a state of turmoil, with politicians not looking after their country but instead trying to fill their own pockets. The former participants of the "Liberation War" of 1919, which resulted in the establishment of an Estonian autonomous country, saw their ideals forgotten. They tried to unite and fight for law and order under their leader, Artur Sirk.

In 1933 Dad had joined the "freedom fighters." Heinz had participated in the Liberation War and was again involved in this movement. Both were in close contact with A. Sirk, flying him and other staff members to different locations of their propaganda meetings. They felt they were doing a good deed for Estonia and at the same time happy to have well paying clients and therefore much needed income.

In 1934 Prime Minister Konstantin Pats took power, declared the freedom movement to be pro-fascist, put Sirk and many of his followers in jail, and accused them of planning a coup-de-etat.

On November 11, 1934 Dad and Heinz von Ungern-Sternberg flew from Viljandi to an airfield near Tallinn, allegedly to transport Sirk to Helsinki. There they were taken into custody and accused of having played a role in the escape of Sirk, who had done so that same day with the help of a well-paid prison guard who disappeared with him.

Sirk managed to escape to Luxembourg, where he was later found dead, assassinated, although authorities called the fall from a third-story window an accident.

Dad and Heinz were held in solitary confinement. They were treated well in jail having many sympathizers. They were allowed to read aviation journals and books. Heinz had his drawing board brought in, and since it was winter and daylight short, he could not see well with his bad eyes. The warden then changed the light bulbs for brighter ones to make it easier for him. Frequent and lengthy interrogations though had to be endured with patience and could not be avoided. They did miss their families and longed to be at home where they knew they were needed.

On February 21, 1935 both, Dad and Heinz were expelled from the Viljandi Air Society under the pretext that they were under arrest and therefore had to be guilty. Open ballots and fear of retaliation by Prime Minister Pats prevented their followers from voting against expulsion. But by expelling them, the Society had to pay back all the expenses paid by Heinz supporting the Society. The sum was 2,397 crowns, more than one-third of their annual budget and quite a financial blow. Average salaries at that time were 50 crowns a month.

Without such aviation fans as Ulrich Brasche and Heinz von Ungern-Sternberg, Viljandi lost its position as the best aviation center in Estonia and the club went bankrupt.

In April of 1935, after about five months of incarceration Dad and Heinz were released free of any charges. The investigation produced no evidence of conspiracy or wrongdoing, and the case was closed.

"You just can't imagine how glad I am to be home again. Those were five long miserable months! I have missed you two so much!" Dad said as he took my mother and me into his arms. "Look at this baby. Rhona has grown so much. She is almost walking." Word spread fast that Dad was back in Viljandi, and family and friends came to see him wanting to hear in his own voice all the details of the last few months. Dad was a good storyteller and he knew how to captivate his audience. No matter the subject, he managed to make it more positive by injecting a few jokes here and there. His humor always showed through.

"It is so good to be at home instead of in that miserable jail cell! And the food is better too," he kept saying.

Dad was relieved that this unpleasant part of his life was over. He took time to enjoy the outdoors, the fresh air. It was spring and the frozen ground had softened. Even though he was not the farmer type, he helped Mom in the garden turning over the dirt and smoothing it out so she could plant her vegetables and flowers. It did his muscles good to be exercised again after months of inactivity. He felt rejuvenated and free.

Many times, as they sat at the table eating lunch or dinner, Mom and Dad made plans for the future, and were often joined by Heinz. They had to come up with a plan soon. The aviation-related jobs were gone, Heinz's pilot's license had been revoked, Dad still had his plane but was not allowed to fly for pay and the Viljandi Air Society had expelled them. The income of these activities had been considerable. Heinz, too, had a family with two children to support. In the meantime, he and Dad had to fall back on the garage, which was profitable enough, but they did not fancy the idea of repairing other people's tractors and farm equipment all their lives. Something different had to come up. Something more challenging.

Dad had made several trips to Germany to buy spare parts for the garage and to develop a feeling for the new technology in motorized vehicles. He used his own car or his BMW motorcycle or the truck from the garage to make the trips because public transportation in Estonia was in its infancy. A railroad connected the big cities, but there was nothing between the smaller towns. The average man had to rely mostly on his own horse and buggy. Few had cars.

Busses were needed. Yes, that was it! Busses and more busses!

"Uli, go talk to the Mercedes Benz people in Germany and see what you can come up with," Heinz said, all exited about that idea. "We have enough space and manpower to start work on at least ten busses. Winter is almost over and the snow is starting to melt. Driving ten "naked" trucks over here will soon be possible."

And so it happened. They came in a long convoy: just the front end with a motor, two wheels, a hard seat for the driver, a long axle, and two double wheels in the back. Those were the future busses for Estonia. Now the work could begin in full force. Quickly the busses took form. The mayor of Viljandi, Mr. August Maramaa, stopped by frequently to observe the progress. Then came the day when the busses were put in service. It was a proud moment for Heinz and my dad. Fifty more of these busses were built over the next two years. During the following years they covered many, many miles helping the citizens to get to their different destinations.

By now it was the winter of 1938. The political climate was changing. Without the opposition of Arthur Sirk, Prime Minister Konstantin Pats had a free hand. Communist infiltration and anti-German agitators from Russia produced an unhealthy atmosphere of suspicion, uncertainty and increased uneasiness. Pats did not combat these sentiments; on the contrary, he helped promote them. It was discovered years later he had been all along secretly on the Russian payroll.

More and more, younger Baltic-Germans were disenchanted with the living conditions in Estonia. The older generation held on to their hopes for better times. Mom's father, who had lost his land and with it his livelihood in 1919, had to seek employment. After a couple of previous jobs, he worked with Heinz and Dad in the garage as a bookkeeper. His health was failing. 1938 was the last Christmas they were to celebrate together. He died the following February and was buried in the family cemetery in Tarvastu.

"I think we have to take some drastic steps now," Dad was saying as he came home from work and took off his muddy boots. It was spring and the ground soggy. "The situation here is going from bad to worse. The officials denied our application to import new spare parts. They don't want us to get ahead. Everywhere you go, it is always *no*, not even a *maybe*."

Mom was just listening. So much had happened since they got married five years earlier. Maybe he was right. Her parents were dead; her brother lived in South America, and her sister she seldom saw. Nothing was impeding a change.

"What do you have in mind? Move someplace else?" she asked as she stopped washing the dishes and dried her hands on her apron. "Do you think it will get really bad? Actually I have heard people talk about an upcoming war. Could that be true? I hope not."

"It is very possible. Russia wants this part of the world in the worst way to get access to the sea."

They both sat in silence for a moment, their thoughts racing in their heads.

"We could go to Germany. I have an aunt in Berlin, Aunt Helene, my dad's sister. She has invited us several times to stay with her," Mom said hesitantly. "Maybe we should think about that."

"I also have an offer from this fellow I met some time ago. He wants me to go to Colombia in South America and fly their commercial planes." Dad countered. "It's just something to keep in mind. Something has to change though. We can't go on like this."

A few restless weeks went by. Should we leave, should we stay, what was the best thing to do?

After a few more unpleasant encounters with the Estonian authorities, the decision was made: they would leave and go to Berlin.

Once in Germany, Dad joined the Air Force voluntarily avoiding a chance of being drafted and getting placed in the infantry. He didn't like much walking and carrying heavy equipment. He wanted to fly but not shoot. With his experience and schooling, he was accepted immediately and trained further. He learned to fly with instruments only and zero visibility, and was introduced to bigger aircrafts.

Once the war started in September of 1939, he was assigned to the Africa Corps under Rommel, the "Desert Fox'. He flew the Junkers JU 52, a large transport plane with three engines. His experience with gliders and the use of air currents helped him cross the Alps with heavy cargo flying from Germany to Italy, North Africa, and Greece, or vice versa.

"Guys, we got hit and lost an engine. We will make it but I need your help," Dad called out one day looking at the instruments. Not all were working. "Everybody get up and stand on the far right side of the plane. We need to level this thing. Everybody ten steps back. No, too much, three forward, a step to the center." As they experimented with their positioning to correct the level of the plane, another crewman crawled to the fuselage to repair and reconnect electrical wires. After some long few minutes, all was in working order and the instruments were back on, but the engine was still dead. They made it to the next military airfield where a new engine was installed and other necessary repairs made. It was just another day of the war.

Being in the Mediterranean area for four years, Dad contracted many tropical diseases and had to be hospitalized frequently. Usually once a year he was sent home for two weeks to recuperate. Those were the only times we saw him. Malaria plagued him for the rest of his life, with high fever attacks lasting several days.

His planes were hit numerous times but he escaped injury. He never crashed or was taken prisoner. He had no fear. He always used to say that fear clouds one's intelligence and leads one to make wrong decisions. Fear is dangerous. A scared soldier is often a dead soldier.

On June 25, 1945, he was discharged from military duty.

He never flew again.

In 2011 a monument was erected in Kullamaa by it's citizens to honor two notable sons of this city: Ulrich Brasche and Alexander Liwentaal, both pilots.

From left to right: Uli (6), Brigitte (8), Juergen (3), and Dieter (10)

Dad's birthplace in Kullamaa

Dad as a young man

Mrs. Karin Brasche, my mom

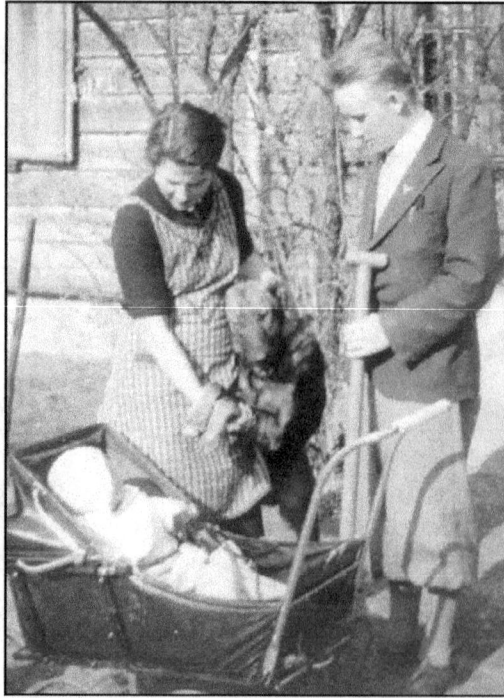

Mom and Dad gardening

Dad and I feeding chicken and Mom and I in Dad's Ford

Heinz third from left and Dad third from right
Both planes were built in Viljandi

Dad and first glider built, waiting on frozen lake to be pulled up by car

I am sitting in our plane and Dad is the first man on the right

Rows of chassis imported from Germany. Dad sitting on the first one

Ready to be transformed into busses

Ready for the next stage

Just about ready

Dad in 1943

Rommel, the Desert Fox in the sands of North Africa

ALEXANDER
LIWENTAAL
3. I 1868 LAUSANNE, SVEITS
15.VIII 1940 HULL, KANADA

ULRICH
BRASCHE
25.XI 1909 KULLAMAA
1.XII 1984 MALLOCO, TSIILI

KULLAMAA KIHELKONNAST PÄRIT
MAAILMA JA EESTI
LENNUNDUSE PIONEERID

AUSTUSEGA KULLAMAA

FIREWORKS

"Let's go to bed now. It is late and also cold. I'll make you some hot chocolate milk," Mom said as she went to the kitchen. "Hopefully this was the last air-raid tonight, because it would be nice to sleep through until morning without being disturbed again."

We had lived for about two years in Berlin with Aunt Helene, a sister of Mom's father. She was a lively, upbeat, petite gray-haired woman. She had been caring for her ailing husband who died not long after we moved in. Aunt Helene had invited us to come to live with her. She left Estonia many years before and wanted to have relatives close to her so she could reminisce about the old times there and learn of the many friends and family members she left behind.

We accepted her invitation a few months before September 1, 1939, the day WW II began. My parents and I left Estonia in anticipation of the war. Experience and foresight told them that it was not safe to stay there any longer. Russia's political development seemed threatening and the Estonian people had become less and less friendly toward people of German origin living there.

We had the use of two large rooms in Aunt Helene's spacious second-story apartment on Hauptstrasse 113 at the corner of Tempelhofstrasse. She lived in a big, three-story U-shaped gray building with a public bomb shelter in the basement. The front facade was richly decorated with cornices and other embellishments. In the center was a patio. A few bushes and small trees in big containers were scattered around to soften the look of the otherwise cold interior stone structure.

Sometimes an organ grinder came by and we listened to his tunes. A few tenants gave him whatever food they had on hand. Others threw coins from their windows. What we kids liked the most was to watch the little brown monkey on a long leash sitting on the organ. He was a nervous little fellow, looking in every direction for coins hitting the ground. He swiftly picked them up, put them in a small pocket in his colorful custom-made pants and lifted his little green felt hat in appreciation.

We were in the second year of the war and the nightly air raids had begun. Now the city had to be dark, no streetlights, no flashy store window displays. All windows had to be covered; no light was allowed to shine through. The city was supposed to be invisible. Police officers walked the streets to make sure everybody adhered to the rules.

Life continued as usual for us with one exception: Now we all had a gas mask and a little suitcase or bag ready to go, packed with the most essential items, or whatever seemed most important to my mother and me. Mine had my little doll and all her clothes Mom had made for her and, of course, my small down pillow without which I could not go to sleep. Mom probably had important papers in hers, together with pictures and cherished mementos.

For me it was nothing unusual or something to be afraid of. Actually, it was kind of exciting. I played with that gas mask and was able to put it on quickly. My parents did not include me in their conversations about the war and since during the day it was mostly peaceful, I didn't think anything of it or gave it much importance. I was in school, had a couple of friends in the building and played with them as seven-year-olds do.

One day, though, I knew that something extraordinary had happened because everybody living in the apartment was sad and teary-eyed.

"Why is everybody crying," I asked my mother as I looked up to her.

"Because Aunt Helene's son went to heaven and everybody misses him."

"Oh….Can I go play now with my friend Anni?"

"Go along, but be back in one hour for lunch."

The only son of Aunt Helene was a pilot, and on his very first mission, his plane was shot down and he was killed. He was only in his early twenties.

As time went by, the air raids became more frequent. Loud sirens, similar to our police car sirens, indicated the beginning, whereas long monotone sounds announced the end, which was usually after sixty to ninety minutes.

Mom and I were always ready to go downstairs to the shelter. Usually I was way ahead of her since I just went in my pajamas and my little robe, whereas

Mom got dressed. We descended that sterile, unfriendly, badly lit emergency staircase holding on to the cold metal railing.

Down below, people streamed in, some wearing just their pajamas or nightgowns and robes. Those were mostly from our building. Others, all dressed up, were partygoers from nearby establishments, and whoever else was in our neighborhood at that time, men, women and children, old and young, heavy-set and skinny, some scared and crying, saying silent prayers, others full of optimistic energy. All were looking for a safe shelter.

Everybody got situated on benches, bunk beds or simply the cement floor, depending on how many shelter seekers had come in. There were people of all walks of life. We were all thrown together by these unusual circumstances, and we all tried to pass the time down there as sanely and cooperatively as possible. Sometimes we could feel the ground tremble and all conversation and movement stopped instantly. We listened. What was it? Where did it hit? How close was it?

One time I had the measles and was not allowed to go down to the bomb shelter. Mom and I stayed in our room. We were dressed in case an emergency arose and we had to leave. We looked out the window when the air attacks came. It was like having our own private theater show. I was fascinated by watching the bright explosions of antiaircraft guns in the dark of the night. Beams of high-powered floodlights swept back and forth across the dark sky searching for enemy planes. They came in precise formation, hundreds at a time. We heard rumbling noises, high-pitched whistles of passing projectiles. Earthshaking explosions made the windows rattle. A rain of small incendiary bombs filled with phosphorus dropped over a big area, causing tremendous fires that were very difficult to put out. Some shots looked like shooting stars in the sky. Others exploded like powder puffs. After what seemed to be an eternity, it became quiet again. The monotone siren announced the end of the air raid and the "fireworks" were over.

Mom never showed any signs of being scared. Her demeanor was calm and reassuring and therefore I was not scared either. She was certainly a very courageous lady who, as a child, had gone through WW I in Estonia and still remembered what had happened then. It was like a repeat of times past. The only difference between the wars was where the bullets came from: in WW I they came from soldiers on the ground and not bombs from airplanes in the sky.

Many years after the war, living in a different continent far away, I heard the siren again. For a long time it startled me. But I knew then, that this time it was to mark twelve noon , in the city. No more "fireworks."

Our Mercedes Dad brought to Germany on his Mercedes truck.
A bomb fell on the garage and all was gone

A LONG JOURNEY SEEKING SAFETY

By 1943 the bombings in Berlin had become so severe that mothers with children had been ordered to leave the city. Whoever did not have a place to go to was assigned one by the authorities. I remember seeing kids at the railroad station with identification tags around their necks showing where they were going. They didn't have anybody to go with them, so they were sent by themselves.

We were lucky to stay with family again. My mother's distant aunt invited us to come and live with her. She had a big sprawling estate in the countryside outside of Reichenbach, close to Görlitz, next to the Polish border. The property was surrounded by a beautiful park, which even included a little lake. The well-maintained orchard was to the side, together with the buildings of a working farm.

The war felt non-existent there. Visiting neighbors came for coffee and cake in their horse drawn carriages. Sometimes we picnicked in the park under some majestic looking old trees. On a few occasions we visited my great-aunt's elderly lady-friend in the next village. The great attraction there was a colorful parrot! To see and hear him talk greatly outweighed the fact that I had to curtsy and kiss the lady's hand.

Mom's sister, Rita, living in Poland at that time had promised to send me a baby goat. When it arrived in a small crate, everybody thought it was a deer because it was brown and small horns were starting to grow. In that part of Germany, goats were white, had no horns and their ears were hanging down, quite a different look. That little pet goat followed me everywhere I went. Unfortunately sometimes it even came inside the house and skipped up the stairs, which was not allowed. It loved the stairs!

We lived happily and peacefully for a couple of years, until March of 1945.

Then one day, my dad, an officer in the German air force, was in the area on military business. Being so close, he made a little detour to see what was happening at the estate, but certainly didn't expect to find us there.

"What, you are still here? I can't believe it!" Those were my dad's words when he walked through the door of my great-aunt's house. We were all sitting around the breakfast table, chatting happily and making plans for the day.

"Why not? What is the matter? What are you doing here?" we exclaimed, some laughingly, some a bit worried, and my mother totally perplexed by his surprise visit.

"Well, you are just about surrounded by the Russian army and need to get out of here immediately!"

For a moment it was silent. "What do you mean, *leave*, we can't leave. We live here!" my great-aunt said. She was a widow in her seventies and this had always been her home. Dad talked to her gently. He explained the consequences of not leaving, like being mistreated or raped by Russian soldiers, possibly sent to Siberia or even, worse, killed. He then offered to stay overnight to help out. After a long silence, and with a deep sigh, she agreed.

A hectic hustle and bustle began. Two wagons hitched to a tractor were parked in front of the house. A carpenter made a roof-like framework over each wagon, and large expensive rugs were placed over them. This way they did not take much room and became useful. Then the loading began. The cook was in the kitchen preparing food to take along. A pig was slaughtered, cut up, and placed in large containers. Several chickens saw their last day. Bread baked in the oven and stew simmered on the stove. Nobody knew how long the trip would take under these circumstances.

By the time the sun rose the next morning, all was ready. My great-aunt and her daughter went through the house one last time, tearfully touching things here and there, wanting to take them, but knowing they could not. She had labeled all the large paintings on the walls indicating the artist and also had added a plea to please be careful with these works of art.

Her diaries, a collection of about 60 books containing her whole life, written in her own hand, had to stay behind, as well as her large dollhouse, my favorite object to look at only, with its beautifully carved furniture, crystal chandeliers, minute porcelain dishes and miniature sterling silver cutlery. It had real paintings on the walls, Belgian lace drapes and tablecloths, knick-knacks and all was of the best material collected over a lifetime. All had to be left behind at the mercy of war.

It was time to leave. The driver took his seat on the tractor, my aunt had a regular chair to sit on and mom, dad, myself and several other people had to find some suitable place to sit on in either of the two wagons.

We were headed for a small village close to Meissen, about 70 miles away. The roads were filled with trucks of all sizes, horse-drawn wagons, cars and people on foot pulling small carts. It was an exodus toward the west. Not many words were spoken. Everybody was preoccupied with his or her own problems, thinking of what they left behind and what the future would bring. Some children were crying. They expressed openly what all were feeling internally.

The going was slow. My dad got us started, but then had to leave and we were on our own. Roads were congested with all kinds of vehicles. It was just about impossible to pass the various slower vehicles. The worst part were the bottlenecks at the crossings of the river Elbe. Bridges were packed and the going slow. It took us over two days traveling day and most of the night to cover those seventy miles and reach our destination, an estate with ample room for everybody.

My great-aunt felt secure again with her friends of many years. Their warm reception and the fact that they had no intensions of leaving either were music to her ears. Forgotten was the plan to continue on for another 200 miles west where friends were expecting us, and where real safety was. The daily sight of squadrons of planes, filled with deadly bombs, flying above us toward their next destination did not deter her. The fact that Dresden, only 20 miles away, a city of great art and no military value, had been leveled just a short time before, did not impress her. That over 100,000 people had perished there did not persuade her either. She had made her decision to stay.

A few days passed then another week and another. My mother became increasingly anxious to leave. The front lines were getting closer and closer. One day while playing outside, I heard cannon fire. I saw a stray plane way above in the sky under attack. It made desperate movements trying to avoid the bullets.

Then it was hit and spiraled down to earth leaving a black plume of smoke behind. I told my mom what I had seen, but that I also had been careful to hide behind the trunk of a tree.

That same day mom asked the lady of the house if she could have the bike she had seen in the garage. She had finally decided to move on. Too much precious time had been wasted already. The situation was not getting any better. Russian troops were advancing steadily. Mother was not scared; she just knew what she had to do to avoid being overrun by the Russian army. WW I experience firmed up her resolve to leave as soon as possible.

"How about going on a long ride?" Mom asked me the next day. I was all for it. That meant that I could ride my small bike, which was my pride and joy. Dad had brought it from Italy and given to me on my birthday. It still looked like new, since I took very good care of it.

Mom packed a small suitcase and strapped it on the back of her bike. A couple of bags hung on her handlebars, and we both had small backpacks. As we said our goodbyes, a plump looking lady named Margarete Rohland approached us, wanting to know if she and her dog could come along. "I will walk fast," she promised. I thought she was ancient, but she probably was only in her mid-fifties. She needed the dog because it was a purebred cocker spaniel with a long pedigree, and the litters of pups were her source of income.

And so the three of us set out on our journey.

My great-aunt, her daughter and granddaughter and all her friends stayed behind, thinking they would be safe. Years later we learned that they lost everything and were taken to a Russian prisoner's camp on the island of Rügen in the Baltic Sea. There they were held in captivity for over a year in miserable conditions.

They definitely had made the wrong choice.

We took shortcuts on back roads following maps and directions penciled on bits of paper. This was unknown territory for us. We wanted to reach the next little town where my mother's aunt had friends and we could spend the night. All went well for a while. We rode the bikes very slowly so the "dog lady" could keep up with us. Since it was more tiring to ride a bike at that slow pace, we decided to do it differently; we rode for a short while and then waited for her to catch up. We did that several times and it worked well.

While we waited for her, we ate a few bites, adjusted the suitcase on my mother's bike and just lay in the grass next to the dirt road. There was little traffic, no noisy speeding cars, and just a few horse-drawn wagons coming home from their chores in the fields. It was spring. Flowers had started to bloom in the meadows. Birds searched for little twigs to make their nests. Bees were collecting pollen and nectar hurrying from one blossom to another. It seemed so peaceful, but the occasional thundering noises in the distance indicated otherwise. They were not weather related. That was not thunder, those were shooting cannons.

"What is taking her so long this time, Mom?" I asked, referring to the lady with the dog.

"Well, I don't know. Let's go back and find her." We rode all the way to the last meeting place. Nothing. There was no trace of her to be found. Since it was getting late in the afternoon and sundown was approaching, my mother decided to continue on. We did not want to be caught by the dark of the night alone on the road. And maybe, just maybe, Margarete had gotten a ride from somebody and was already at our destination point.

After a few kilometers, we arrived at the big manorial farmhouse. As it turned out, we were not the only ones passing through. Several families with horse-drawn wagons were parked in the front feeding their animals. A group of people was inside the house. Some were talking about past experiences and close calls; others discussed the best routes to the West. But nowhere could we find Margarete. What had happened to her? Nobody had seen her and she was not easy to miss with her dog.

We were given a small room with a bed. What luxury! That was to be one of the last beds at our disposal for a long time, but we did not know that then. We slept soundly until about midnight, when a loud commotion in the hallway woke us up. The missing lady and her dog had arrived! Somehow she had gotten lost. After walking and walking for a long time, she realized that the thundering noise was getting louder and louder. She was heading in the wrong direction, toward the military lines instead of away from them! It took her all that time to get back and actually find us. I thought an angel must have watched over her.

We stayed another day to give her time to recuperate from that ordeal. In the meantime, my mother had met a petite and energetic lady at the house, who was there by her self and was also "ancient" in my young eyes. By coincidence, she happened to be from Estonia, as was my mother, and that immediately bonded them. They both knew the Russians well and wanted to move on as soon as possible.

The next morning, after a hearty breakfast served by our generous hosts, our bags replenished with food, accompanied by good wishes, we set out on the next leg of our journey. What a strange group we were: Two older women on foot, a ten-year-old kid on a small bike, my mother on a regular bike with that slipping and sliding suitcase tied to it, and the black cocker spaniel.

That suitcase was soon thrown into a ditch. It just did not want to stay in place and was not worth keeping for all the trouble it caused. We should have taken a soft-sided sack. Well, live and learn. At that time one could find lots of discards on the sides of the road. Things get heavier and heavier the longer one walks, and quickly lose their importance. So now there we were, with just the clothes we were wearing and some bags with ever so important food and water. But we had determination.

Before my dad left to return to his post, he and my mother had agreed on five addresses of friends and relatives where they would look for each other. It was the only way to reunite in these uncertain times. The first address was Weissenfels, about 70 miles west as the crow flies. That's were we headed now.

This time we stayed together, no more riding ahead and waiting. We hung all the bags on the bikes handlebars and started pushing. The lady that had joined us at the last stop was probably in her early sixties. She was a slender, petite, but very energetic person, who had seen better days, as had we all. She was ready to conquer any obstacle.

"Let me push your bike and you can take the dog for a while," she offered. Never having done that before, she frequently hit her ankles on the pedals, but soon was a pro. I held the leash for a while, so the other lady could walk freely. This dog was one of those that pull so hard on the leash that they make hoarse, choking noises, gasping for air. Luckily she quit that bad habit after a week or so. There were so many new things to sniff, that she forgot all about pulling ahead. Now we had to yank her to make her follow us.

The next few days we came through several little villages. We traveled on smaller back roads, away from heavy traffic. People were friendly and tried to help us as much as they could, indicating the best ways to get from one little town to the next. We slept mostly in barns on big heaps of straw covered with a blanket. It was soft and warm, and smelled like "country." Roosters awakened us early in the morning. Dogs barked, sensing our cocker spaniel.

Our next obstacle was the river Mulde. As with the river Oder, all bridges were jammed by vehicles of all sorts. In the distance we saw uniformed individuals patrolling and questioning people, and since we did not know for sure what this was all about, we did not want to take a chance by continuing on. They could have sent us back or taken us somewhere, who knows. These were uncertain times and one had to be suspicious of everything.

As we stood on the side of the road deliberating what to do next, a young friendly looking police officer approached my mother after surveying our little group.

"Can I help you?" he asked. "Do you want to get to the other side?" As my mother nodded, he walked a few steps ahead and motioned her to follow him. We saw them talking and then he was writing something on a piece of paper. A few more words were exchanged and he left.

My mother came back and we could see that she was happy.

"He gave me directions for where to cross the river!" she exclaimed jubilantly. "There is a factory a few kilometers downstream that has a footbridge over the Mulde. We just have to make sure to cross when nobody is around."

We took a small, narrow footpath that followed the shoreline. Tall trees stood on both sides with a great amount of underbrush. Ferns grew in the shade; moss covered the ground. It smelled of humidity and mushrooms and the air was still and heavy. We walked silently for quite a while. Then the path became rocky and gradually turned uphill. That meant we were getting close to the factory on the other side of the river, according to that police officer's diagram. As we rested, my mother went ahead by herself to check it out, leaving her bike behind. She wasn't gone long, when she came back with a smile on her face.

"We are in luck. It seems that the factory is closed, not a soul in sight," she said. "But the downhill path is steep and slippery from here on."

She made several trips down to the bridge. First she took the bikes, which she left in the bushes. Then she came for me and the dog, and lastly she fetched the ladies one at a time. We could ill afford an accident at this stage of our travel. It would have been disastrous! The bridge was wooden, narrow, and just wide enough for a person to cross pushing a bike. Six or seven steps led up to the beginning, and at the end the same amount of steps down. The river itself was not very wide or deep, but had a very strong current.

We stood all together and looked around. There was still nobody in sight. Then we crossed quickly, treading softly, avoiding making much noise. One could never be too cautious. Once over the bridge and out of the factory grounds, we sighed with relief. We had made it. Now we just had to find the next little village where we could spend the night.

We always had to memorize the names of the villages we came through. One was not allowed to leave one settlement for more than a certain amount of miles in radius. Based on that, we *lived* in many places but just for a few hours or one night. It all depended on how fast we walked and how many villages we came through.

We had reached the first address in Weissenfels. Dad was not there, but we were not disappointed. It was too soon; the war was still in full force. I can't remember who those people were, but we left word with them that our next stop would be Jena, roughly 35 miles southwest from there.

About three to four weeks had passed, since the beginning of our journey when we left my great-aunt's estate. The going was slow. More and more often, German authorities stopped us, wanting to know where we were coming from and where we were headed. One of these encounters became frightening

"Do you have any weapons with you?" the policeman asked. "It is against the law to carry any, you know!"

Mom was just about to reply negatively, when the dog-lady shouted out "Yes, she has a pistol. Just look," as she pointed to the bag hanging on the bike's handlebar.

We stood frozen to the ground. Why did she say that? What would he do now? An awkward moment passed, then Mom slowly reached into her bag, pulled out a small handgun, and, handing it to the man, she explained in a low, but firm voice: "We are Baltic Germans fleeing from the Russians. Had you been in our shoes, you too would have had one in your bag for safety. We were not going to fall into their hands alive. Siberia is not an option for us!"

Then there was silence. We didn't even breathe. Finally, the man took the gun and, without saying a word, looked at my mom, and signaled us to move on. That was a close call! When we were out of sight, the dog-lady began to cry. She was shaking, her hands trembling. After a while she regained her composure and apologized. I guess her nerves were stretched thinner than ours. We felt very sorry for her.

"Did you hear, that the war is about to end?' we were asked by a passer-by as we walked along a road. We were dumbfounded. Could that really be true?

"Who told you that? Was it published somewhere or did you hear that on the radio, on BBC?" my mother asked. The man just grinned without answering, waved and continued on his way. "He probably heard it on the BBC London and didn't want to admit to it." Mom commented. It was forbidden to listen to that station, but many people did anyway, hidden behind closed doors and the radios on low volume. We heard so many different stories these days that it was difficult to know the truth.

We had reached Jena and gone on to Saalfeld, always leaving word for Dad. Much time was spent now in finding places to stay overnight. We always started to search for one early in the afternoon. If we were not successful, then the mayor of the village or small town where we were at was our last resort. He gave us an official order form that indicated an address where they had to take us in.

Our two companions were making plans to go their own separate ways to reach their respective destinations with relatives and friends. The Russian danger had diminished and on May 7, 1945, the war finally came to an end. Not much changed for us though. We still had to reach the last two meeting places, the last two of the five addresses.

Then one day we encountered the first American soldiers. They didn't pay any attention to us, like we were nonexistent, but I certainly looked them over curiously. There was nothing special about them, just people like us only in different uniforms and speaking English. One soldier stood out though: he was different, he was black. I had never seen a black person before, only some depicted in my storybooks.

The rest of the trip was somewhat uneventful. The ladies had left us and we were on the way to Sonneberg, always going south, or south west.. There we were forced to stay for a week: I had developed a nasty cold, combined with asthma and we were unable to continue. I still remember that soft, cozy bed they put me in, with a down comforter to sleep on and another one as a cover.

For the rest of our long journey we used other modes of transportation, having left our bikes behind. We walked, hitch-hiked and rode buses when available. Then, finally, we reached Hohenfeld, our destination. This was the last address. Luckily we could stay with the Kuhnert Family, since they had a guest room we could use. Dad's sister was married to Mrs. Kuhnert's brother.

Now it was just a matter of waiting for Dad. We didn't know where he was or what had happened to him after we separated at the onset of our journey.

Weeks went by. I became friends with the four children in the house; we played but also had chores to do. Mom helped out where needed. Meals were a big affair. Mr. and Mrs. Kuhnert, his mother, the four children and mom and myself, all nine of us were sitting around a large table. I learned to eat quickly; otherwise there was nothing left for seconds. Then one day, at the beginning of July, we had just finished our meal and still sat around the table. The door opened slightly and a head peeked through.

"Hello, how are you all?" a very familiar voice said.

It was my dad.

CERTIFICATE OF DISCHARGE

PERSONAL PARTICULARS

ALL ENTRIES WILL BE MADE IN BLOCK LATIN CAPITALS AND WILL BE MADE IN INK OR TYPE* SCRIPT.	25247

SURNAME OF HOLDER___BRASCHE_____ DATE OF BIRTH___25.11.1909____
DAY, MONTH, YEAR

CHRISTIAN NAME____ULRICH_____ PLACE OF BIRTH___GOLDENBECK/ESTLAND___

CIVIL OCCUPATION___MOTOR DRIVER AND____ FAMILY STATUS - SINGLE Ø
PILOT   MARRIED   MARRIED
HOME ADDRESS_____HOHENFELD/WUERZBURG____ WIDOW(ER)
BAYERN_____ DIVORCED   ONE
                          NUMBER OF CHILDREN WHO ARE MINORS, ONE

I HEREBY CERTIFY THAT TO THE BEST   *extended to Fürstenfeldbruck bei*
OF MY KNOWLEDGE AND BELIEF THE PAR-   *München*   ALLIED
TICULARS GIVEN ABOVE ARE TRUE.   EXPEDITIONARY
I ALSO CERTIFY THAT I HAVE READ AND   FORCE
UNDERSTOOD THE "INSTRUCTIONS TO   MILITARY
PERSONNEL ON DISCHARGE"(CONTROL FORM D.1)   GOVERNMENT
                 SIGNATURE OF HOLDER...... *Ulrich Brasche*   BY
                                                              stamp

NAME OF HOLDER IN
BLOCK LATIN CAPITALS___ULRICH BRASCHE_____

II
MEDICAL CERTIFICATE

DISTINGUISHING MARKS___NONE_____

DISABILITY, WITH DESCRIPTION____NONE_____

MEDICAL CATEGORY_____

I CERTIFY THAT TO THE BEST OF MY KNOWLEDGE
AND BELIEF THE ABOVE PARTICULARS RELATING
TO THE HOLDER ARE TRUE AND THAT HE IS NOT
VERMINOUS OR SUFFERING FROM ANY INFECTIOUS
OR CONTAGIOUS DISEASE.
                 SIGNATURE OF MEDICAL OFFICER___*Joseph R Saab*___
                 NAME AND RANK OF MEDICAL OFFICER
                 IN BLOCK LATIN CAPITALS____JOSEPH R SAAB CAPT MC___

III
THE PERSON TO WHOM THE ABOVE PARTICULARS
REFER WAS DISCHARGED ON_____25 JUN 1945___
                             (DATE OF DISCHARGE)

FROM THE X____AIRFORCE_____

RIGHT
THUMBPRINT

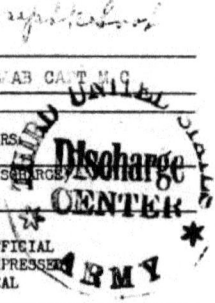

OFFICIAL
IMPRESSED
SEAL

CERTIFIED BY_____
NAME, RANK AND
APPOINTMENT OF ALLIED
DISCHARGING OFFICER___*Ulrich*___

Ø DELETE THAT WHICH IS INAPPLICABLE
* INSERT "ARMY" "NAVY" "AIR FORCE"
  "VOLKSSTURM", OR PARA MILITARY
  ORGANIZATION, e.g. "RAD", "SPK", etc.

ROBERT L CHRIST CAPT INF
IN BLOCK LATIN CAPITALS

(WHEN PRINTED THIS FORM WILL BE IN ENGLISH AND GERMAN)

HOHENFELD – 1945

From 1945 until 1949 we lived in Hohenfeld, a quaint little village on an upward sloping terrain next to the river Main. A cobblestone road wound through it and old, half-timbered houses stood on both sides. It was a really small village, not more than ten blocks long and with only four or five side streets.

A big hexagonal fountain stood in the center of town where most people had to get their water. Very few had a well and pump on their property. Tall bucket-like containers were filled with that precious liquid and carried home on one's back, like a backpack. It was a heavy load and one had to develop a certain rhythm when walking to avoid the water slopping over, right into one's neck. Needless to say, water was not wasted and a hot bath in a tin tub was only a weekly affair on Saturdays, if at all. This fountain was sort of a gathering point. While the water containers were filling, the latest news and gossips were exchanged. The water from the fountain flowed into a lower rectangular trough for animals to drink.

It was a farming community with just a couple of grocery stores, two restaurants, the bakery and a church. The schoolhouse, a newer building, was at one end of town and a little chapel next to the cemetery stood on a hill overlooking the village. Any news of the town leadership, engagement and marriage announcements, or information of upcoming special functions were displayed on a glass-covered bulletin board, that was attached to the outside wall of the restaurant, close to the big fountain. If there was an urgent message, a man walked through town ringing a big bell to call people's attention, and every block or so he read his communication out loud.

We stayed with our friends, Addi and Ursula Kuhnert. Addi was an author and a playwright for German movies and spent his days behind closed doors in his study. A big desk stood in the middle of the room and all the walls were covered with books. It was his sanctuary, and kids were not allowed to enter unless they were sent there specifically to receive a scolding for misbehavior or some other infraction of rules. Very seldom was it for something pleasant. The Kuhnert's had a big house with a large vegetable patch in the back, a few fruit trees, a henhouse for chickens, and some turkeys and ducks.

I can still hear aunt Ursula's voice calling out to me: "Can you go and find the turkeys?" Apparently they did not like the henhouse and in the evening perched in the surrounding trees. This became my daily chore

A large portion of the garden was planted with tobacco. The plants were very tall and we kids had to break off the big leaves at the bottom and string them up to dry. The smokers exchanged recipes for the best method and ingredients for "curing" the leaves. After the leaves were finely cut, I rolled the cigarettes and became quite proficient at it.

Dad was discharged from the Air Force on June 25th. Never having been taken prisoner, he had to present himself to the American authorities who issued the necessary papers. One paragraph, signed by Joseph R. Saab, Capt. MC., said: "He is not verminous or suffering from any infectious or contagious diseases." We chuckled a lot about that.

The war had disrupted our lives. We lost everything in Estonia and what little we had in Germany. A bomb hit the garage in Berlin, where we kept our Mercedes. We had nothing. It was time to think about a new beginning. In Estonia Dad built single-engine airplanes and gliders and then taught people how to fly them. That was not a possibility now, and he had to search for other ways of making a living.

He started to build radios. It was a slow beginning, having to read and learn a lot until the wee hours of the morning. But his interest had always been there. As a young boy he played with the beginnings of today's modern radios, the very simple quartz mechanism. He sat on the steps of his father's church and entertained the worshippers on their way to hear his father's sermon. Many times they paused too long arriving late, and Dad got a scolding.

After making the decision to build radios, he had to locate a carpenter who could make the cabinets. He tried several, until he found a master of his trade. His work was beautiful. To this date I have a little box he made for me, with a different colored wood inlay in the lid.

The radios Dad made were mostly traded for food, clothing, and other necessities or cigarettes. Cigarettes were the currency of the black market. Everything had a price in cartons of cigarettes during those days. The barter system was flourishing.

I remember that once we had a whole sack of potatoes and Mom learned how to make wonderful cakes with them, we thought then. A little seven-year-old neighbor boy, whose parents were farmers and not hurting for food, had a piece. After he took a bite, he gave the rest back to Mom and said, "My mother bakes better cakes." I guess everything is a matter of opinion.

Summer was coming to an end and I started school. First to eighth grade were all in one classroom, but we were not that many kids. Still, what a nightmare for the teacher! But all went well. I cannot recall any unpleasant incidents. That year we didn't have any books, paper or other supplies, just our black slates. By the following year the situation improved and we had to catch up. All schoolchildren in that part of Germany had to repeat the previous school year because of time missed due to the war.

Soon fall turned into winter. It was getting cold. Snow blanketed the village and the river Main froze over from shore to shore. Christmas was upon us. In the morning of Christmas Eve, we all went to the nearby woods to look for a tree. Once brought back home, it disappeared behind closed doors. Nobody was allowed to peek or go into that room until the celebration began in the evening. We kids waited anxiously. And then finally the door opened.

What a sight! The star topped tree reached the ceiling! It was decorated with cookies, chocolates, gilded walnuts and glittery tinsel. Its many real wax candles lit up the room. The flames flickered with the moving air and made interesting shadows on the walls and ceiling. The room smelled like pine. Below, under the tree, were the unwrapped presents, a little grouping for each child. We were taking in the sight of this splendor and didn't mind singing a few Christmas songs. With "Oh Tannenbaum" and "Silent Night" our little repertoire came to an end.

Excitement and happiness were in the air. For a while all the heartache, suffering and unpleasantness of the last few months were forgotten.

Life was good again

Hohenfeld on the river Main

Chapel sits on the hill with vineyards on the slopes

Ferry crossing the river

Main street and fountain

"We did it, we did it! We can move to a bigger place!" Mom called out all excited. She so much wanted more room for us, and a stove to cook on. She wanted independence and to be her own boss. Now she found it. The house was on the other side of town, going uphill on a side street, away from the main road. Two rooms on the second floor were available. One would be our bedroom and the other the living room, Dad's workstation and kitchen. And yes, it had a wood-burning stove with a small oven for baking. A toilet was in the hallway between the two rooms. There was no bathtub or shower, but we had to live with that.

The house belonged to a farmer and his wife. They lived downstairs, their daughter with husband and son lived upstairs in three rooms, and we had the other two. A barn was attached to one side of the house, where they had a couple of cows and four pigs. Hay and straw were kept in the rafters above. At a right angle to the barn stood a woodshed and a row of smaller enclosures for tools, farm equipment and workbenches.

What mostly caught the eye though, was a big pile of manure in front of the barn. It sat in a cemented excavation of maybe five feet in depth and was surrounded by a one-foot tall cement border. These piles of manure were the pride of all farmers. The bigger the pile, the more animals they had and, therefore, the better off they were. But they did stink when disturbed, especially when the fields were readied for the next crop and fertilized with all that good material. The fields were not all connected, but spread out over a large area. One piece was here, another there and a few in between. The cows were ordinary milk cows, but they also had to pull wagons to the fields and bring in the harvest. Sometimes a farmer would use a cow and a horse together, which looked kind of odd, but it seemed to work. They learned how to adjust to each other. The human race could take a lesson!

Our bedroom window looked out onto the yard. Through the two windows in the other room we had a beautiful view over the meadows, and the vineyards on the slopes of the hill reaching the cemetery and little chapel. Since the house was the last one on the street, the view was totally unobstructed and endless.

Mom was setting up her little household. She needed everything. Somehow we rounded up beds and other furnishings, pots and pans, a few dishes and some silverware. People were so helpful and good-hearted. It was amazing. If they could not give it to us, they let us use it until a replacement was found and we could give it back. And, of course, we always did.

Dad found a part-time job in an electronic business in Kitzingen, a city up river, about two and a half miles away. It was a good size town with a high school for girls and one for boys. One just had to follow the cobblestone road, which ran through our village. But that was the longer way. One could also take a small ferryboat and a man took people to the other side of the river Main. Coming back one just had to yell or ring a big bell. There was no timetable; necessity was the driving force. The ferry operated as long as there was daylight.

For two years I took that ferry together with two other girls from Hohenfeld, Ilse and Hannelore, as we were going to high school in Kitzingen. It was the only one in the area. In wintertime, when the river Main froze over, we crossed the ice trying to find a more or less even path amid the ice floes, which had been randomly pushed one over the other before freezing into a solid sheet. In the morning, when it was really cold, I stopped by at the bakery and bought 2 small rolls and held them in my pocket to warm my hands.

We developed a quick pace walking the 2.5 miles to school every day along the railroad tracks and then entering the town itself. Our few books we carried in backpacks. Some times, on our way home, we found pieces of coal that had fallen off the trains. We gathered all we could find since those were a much-appreciated commodity and our moms were happy to receive them for use in their stoves. In those days nothing was wasted.

Dad used his bike to go to work, the same bike on which he rode into our little village the previous summer. Sometimes he brought work home, simple things I could do. I remember the day when I had to make a certain electronic part by winding fine wire onto 200 cores of delicate and flaky asbestos. It was not unusual back then to handle asbestos, but in today's world they might put Dad in jail for child endangerment. Times change!

I was looking forward to little jobs like that. Often I was at home in bed recovering from a cold and asthma. I had read all the books we had and was bored.

One year, Hannelore, Ilse and I staged a little show for family, friends and neighbors. It was Rumpelstilzchen, the fairy tale. We wrote our own scripts, had a few props, but mainly we made use of a lot of imagination. For our spectators we brought chairs to the basement and warmed the place up with a good fire in a stove that happened to be there. Several families donated the wood.

The show must have been a success, because fifty-five years later, when I visited Hohenfeld for the first time since I left, they still remembered that play.

Dad was still making and trading radios, but it was getting harder and harder to find the needed vacuum tubes. New production of them had not started. But even so, one day all three of us had handmade leather shoes with pretty topstitching. They were much needed and came just in time for winter.

During the war we had plenty of food. Everything was available, but now it was a different story. We were issued food-rationing stamps every month. So much flour, so many eggs, fat hardly any, sugar, and so on. It was never enough. We were lucky, though, to live in a small community of farmers. The news of a vegetable or fruit sale by one of them spread like wildfire. Many times we stood in line to buy whatever edibles they were selling. Even sugar beets were appreciated. We cut them in small pieces and simmered those for hours. The final result was sweet syrup. Meat was hardly ever obtainable.

We thought we were smart and got ourselves a rabbit. They multiply rapidly and would be a good source of protein. Dad built a cage and I could keep it downstairs in the yard. Every day I gathered food for it in the nearby meadows. Soon we had eight little rabbits and they were so cute. They became our pets. When they were full-grown, we gave them all away. How could we even think of eating them!

Often we went to the nearby woods to gather mushrooms and berries. It was public land and we did not trespass. One of these outings did not go so well. We were a small group: Mom, aunt Lia, who was Dad's sister, and several children. We were on our way home. Suddenly a man appeared from nowhere and attacked us with his bare fists, knocking out two of Mom's front teeth.

The baskets with our laboriously gathered berries and mushrooms were flung aside. He was screaming and yelling that we had trampled over his crops, which was not the case. Then, as suddenly as he had come, he left mumbling to himself. Later we found out that he had mental problems due to a bullet in his brain. Relatives paid dentist costs and he was put temporarily in an institution.

He was another sad casualty of war, as was the man who came home by the end of 1947 after several years of Russian imprisonment. The whole village gave him a big welcome. They wined and dined him. He was a celebrity and he enjoyed it, happy to be home again. But shortly after, he died of a heart attack. His frail body could not take the sudden change in nourishment and all the commotion without a slow adjustment. It was too much too quick.

Even though the war was over, the effects were still felt and would be for many years to come.

Mom chatting while waiting for her turn

Two containers several times a day, uphill

Left to right Mrs. and Mr. Schneider (Walter's grandparents), Rhona, Ulrich
Brasche, my dad, Mrs. and Mr. Knauf (Walter's parents)
Below Mrs. Schneider

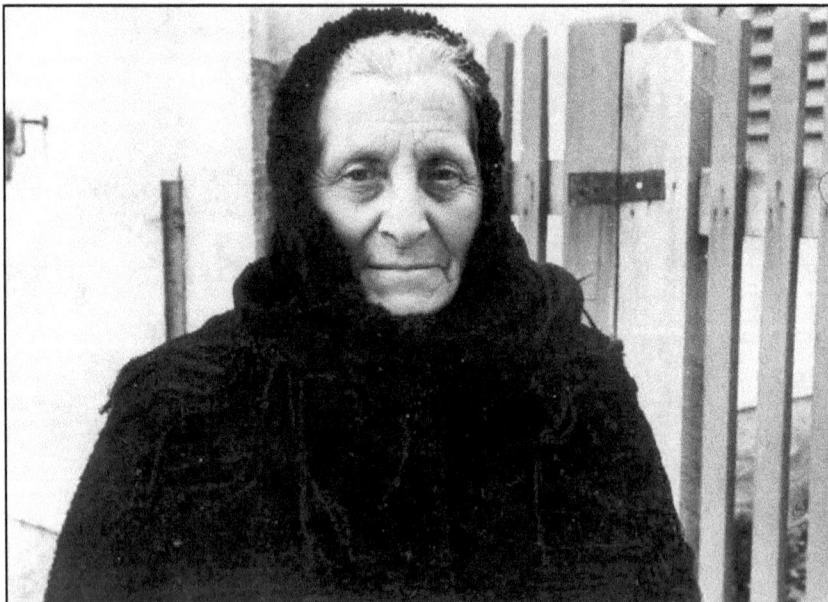

Mr. and Mrs. Knauf and son Walter

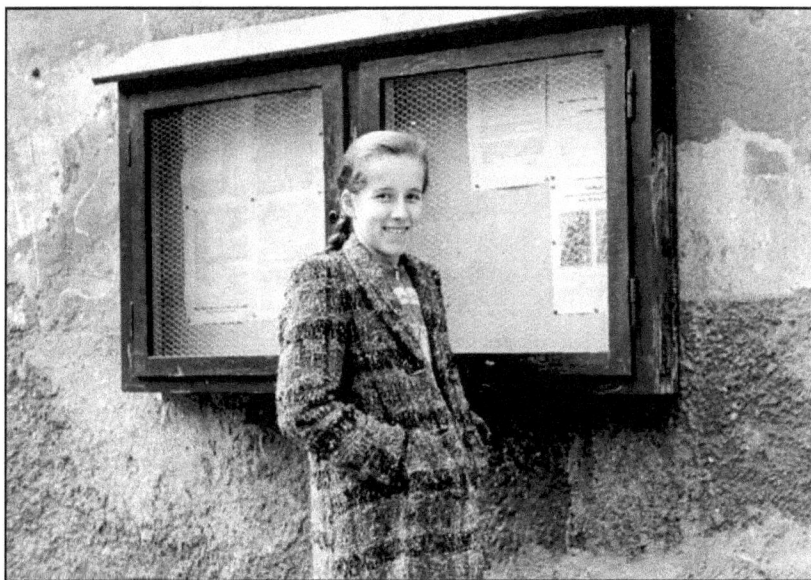

Rhona in front of bulletin board

Rhona and her cat

CHANGE OF HEMISPHERES

"What would you say if we made plans to move to South America? Would you like that, would you want to go?" my parents asked me one day late in the year 1948.

"Sure, why not?" I answered without hesitation. "What country exactly did you have in mind, and when would we leave?"

"We will go to Chile," they replied. Of course, I should have known. Chile was where Mom's brother was living. He had emigrated in 1927 during the big depression in Germany. He was well established now and twice had sent us a "Care" package (short for Cooperative for Americans Remittance to Europe).

"We will leave once we have all the papers and documents together, which probably will take several months." Dad commented.

I was fourteen years old and had lived in several places by then. My first five years in Estonia I hardly remembered. Life in Berlin was nice. I recalled visiting the zoo, where a rhino didn't close his gigantic mouth until onlookers had thrown several heads of lettuce into it. We went to a circus, which was a big novelty for me. I started school. Then the bombings began in Berlin and we moved in with my mother's aunt in Silesia. She lived in the country close to Görlitz, not far from the Polish border. That proved not to be a good choice. After a couple of years there, we had to escape again, leaving everything we owned behind.

And during all this time, we saw my dad only once or maybe twice a year. He had enlisted voluntarily in the Air Force and was with the Africa Corps under Rommel's command in Italy, North Africa and later in France. Now we had lived in Lower Franconia a little over three years, about a two-hour drive southeast from Frankfurt. It was nice, but could and should be much better. So why not search for it?

Chile sounded interesting. Most people didn't even know where it was, had never heard of it! Must be somewhere on the other side of the world. Were Indians living there? Were there wild and dangerous animals? We had many good laughs about the questions we were asked.

Progress obtaining the necessary papers, permits, proof of just about everything was slow. Documents had been lost during the war and needed to be replaced. Affidavits had to be gathered and witnesses produced. It was bureaucracy at its best. Finally in early 1949 things began to run smoother. Just a few more documents, stamps, signatures, and the mandatory shots and vaccinations against contagious diseases were needed and we could be on our way.

Twice a week I had to take a little commuter train to Würzburg. We had found a doctor there who was treating me for my asthma by giving me some shots. On those days I missed school. I really didn't mind at all, but it was not easy to keep up with the other students.

"Dad and I were thinking that maybe you should skip school all together until we get to Chile. What do you think about that?" Mother said one day in February. "It is cold, the river is frozen over and you don't have to walk the two miles plus to school. We'd rather have you see the doctor three times a week now instead of two."

Needless to say I was the happiest kid on earth in that moment. We had figured that maybe by April we could embark on our trip. That meant two months of vacation! Yes! Not that I hated school, but this was good. This was very good!

Slowly we started to prepare for the trip. Mom bought a new suit for herself with fur trim and a hat to go with it. I was fitted for a coat and mom bought material with a small flower print for a dress for me. It was all so exciting and I loved it! Especially since in the last few years I had only hand-me-downs in drab, dark colors. New material was scarce therefore several pieces of used clothing were dyed the same shade. That produced more material of the same color, which then could be sewn into something new. But the color was always going from dark to darker.

During all this time we were waiting for the still needed papers allowing us to leave Germany, a transit visa for France and the immigration visa from the Chilean embassy. Why do they take so long I kept thinking to myself? How hard is it to sign a piece of paper and stamp it. But, then, these were not normal times.

There was a big onslaught of diverse petitions. Many people wanted to leave to join other family members or simply to leave bad memories behind and start a new life. And there were also those who wanted to escape the law, people with shady backgrounds or with something to hide. All had to be sorted out and I guess that took time.

"I think this is it! I think this is what we are waiting for!" my dad said one day as he was holding a very official looking envelope in his hands. The mailman had just delivered it.

"Well, open it. What are you waiting for? Hurry!" Mom and I were jumping up and down. Could that really be it? What suspense! Our hearts were beating. Dad sat down, and with a knife, he carefully opened the envelope. Slowly he pulled out the content. He was right! It was all there. Everything we needed. Finally!

Now we could actually get train tickets and book passage on a ship that would take us to Chile. Airfares were too expensive in those days. My uncle had made tentative reservations on the "Reina del Pacifico" for the end of April, arriving in Valparaiso on May 20th. We were in time.

Now that everything was decided and we were going to leave, we went to see my aunt Rita, mom's sister who lived in the outskirts of Kassel. They were very close and mom wanted to see her one more time. We didn't know then, that a couple of years later she and Uncle Harry would follow us to Chile.

Upon our return and after a few more goodbyes we started to pack our belongings. All fit into three suitcases. We traveled light. The furniture and stove we left behind for somebody else to use. We had been helped and now maybe we could return the favor.

Then came the day for us to leave. Our landlady and her son Walter accompanied us to the train station. Pretty soon the big monster of a locomotive could be seen in the distance as it approached the station. As the coaches slowly rolled in we saw the one that in big letters had written on it: La Rochelle. That's us; we were going to France.

The big locomotive came to a halt, releasing blasts of steam. As the train stopped, coaches bumped into each other, adding to the noise. Doors slammed as they were opened and porters emerged from each car. Steps were placed in front of the doors for easier access. Our friends and we were the only group of persons on the platform. Apparently not many people were traveling. We said our last good byes and, accompanied by their good wishes, climbed into the La Rochelle coach. Soon the train set its wheels into motion and we were on our way. Our trip had started. The adventure began!

For a while we sat quietly in our seats, absorbing our surroundings. This was a big moment. One does not embark on a trip like this frequently. What would we encounter? What had the future in store for us? Dad checked all the documents one more time. It was all there, hopefully! Requirements had changed several times before and one could never be sure.

"Let's have a sandwich, I am hungry!" I exclaimed. Mom reached into the overhead compartment and retrieved a large bag. We had prepared a few snacks to take along and our friends surprised us with some more goodies. Now we had more than enough.

Before long they came to check our tickets. That was no problem. But would the French border personnel find our other papers acceptable? In a few hours we were to find out. The food, the warm air and the monotonous clickety-clack of the moving train soothed the exhausting hectic nervousness of the last few days, and we fell asleep.

"Papers, please!" a loud voice called out. We awoke instantly. This is it. This is the French border control.

"Here are all the papers we were told to obtain." Dad said, handing the uniformed man the requested documents. "The exit permit, the French visa and immigration approval from Chile, they are all here."

The railroad official looked them over, then again and again. Did he hold us in suspense on purpose? Finally he handed them back, said "Tres bien, bon voyage," and stepped over to the next group of passengers. How relieved we were!

Soon we arrived in Paris. It was a good thing that Mom spoke some French. We checked into a small hotel. From our window we could see the Basilica of the Sacre Coeur (Sacred Heart) gleaming white above the city. The following three days we spent sightseeing. The Eiffel Tower offered a wonderful view of the city from above. Champs-Elysees leading to the Arc de Triumphe was bigger and wider than anything I had seen before. We also visited Notre Dame, Napoleon's Tomb and of course the Louvre. After a long day of walking, we collapsed in one of those charming sidewalk cafes, rested our feet and did some people watching. It didn't seem much different from home, except for the language. They had won the war, yet it seemed that they were not better off than we were.

Le Havre, the port where we were to board the *Reina del Pacifico*, was only about one hundred miles away from Paris. We had to be there the following morning.

Our worries were unfounded. Again all our papers passed inspection and we were allowed to board the ship. People were everywhere looking for their assigned accommodations. It was nervous time, tempers flared. Why did they push and shove? It was not a "first-come-first-serve" situation! Mom, two other females, and I had to share a small cabin with two bunk beds somewhere in the bottom of the pit. Dad was placed with the men. There was no room in any of the cabins for luggage. All suitcases and bags were kept separately in a big storage room supervised by a sailor. Upon request he brought them out, one could take or return items, and then he took them back from where they came.

Obviously, we were traveling third class but still in more comfort than the emigrants on the Mayflower. By mid-day all passengers had found their cabins, had settled in and were heading for the deck. Nobody wanted to miss the departure. It was a cool but sunny day, visibility was excellent and many of the passengers had a camera on hand.

The *Reina del Pacifico* was impressive with her two smokestacks. She was built in 1931 and sailed under English colors between Liverpool and the west coast of South America via the Panama Canal. During WW II she had troopship duties. In 1947 she was returned to the builders for refurbishment and resumed her South American service in 1948. She had a displacement of 17,000 tons and carried 900 passengers plus crew.

Mom, Dad and I found a place right on the railing with an unobstructed view. We were high above the water. We could see that preparations were underway to take to the sea. The ship vibrated slightly as the engines warmed up. The ocean water began to churn as if it was boiling. The anchors on both sides of the ship were hauled up. Slowly the vessel edged away from the mooring, turned and headed for the open sea. We watched for a long time as the city and then the coastline disappeared in the horizon. It was time to turn around and look to the future.

What would it bring?

Waiting for the train to La Rochelle-France

Reina del Pacifico

1931

(Albatros AL-123)

- *Type:* Passenger
- *Displacement:* 17,707 tons
- *Dimensions:* 574 x 76 ft.
- *Machinery:* Burmeister & Wain diesels, quadruple screws = 18 knots
- *Passengers:* 888 (280 first class, 162 second class, 446 third class)

- *Builder:* Harland & Wolff, Limited, Belfast, Northern Ireland, 1931

- *Service:* Built for Pacific Steam Navigation Company. Liverpool-west coast of South America via Panama Canal. Voyage to Valparaiso in 1936 completed in record 25 days. Troopship duties, 1939-46. These included expedition to, and reembarkation from Norway, 1940; trips to Suez via Cape Town; transportation of the 4th Indian Division from Egypt to Port Sudan for the attack on Ethiopia, Jan 1941. Landing craft added for North African invasion, and transported elements of 1st U.S. Division to Oran assault, Nov 1942. Transported elements of 51st Highland Division to landings at Avola, Sicily, Jul 1943. Later trips between Britain and Bombay, East Africa, and the Pacific. Repatriation duties 1946, and returned to builders for refurbishment, 1947. During sea trials, engine room accident killed 28 personnel, Sep 1947. Resumed South American service, 1948-58. Scrapped in Wales, 1958.

CROSSING THE ATLANTIC

The vast ocean lay in front of us. Stark white cumulus clouds billowed above us contrasting beautifully with the blue of the sky. A few seagulls circled above the ship looking for scraps of food thrown overboard or small fish that ventured too close to the surface of the sea. Soon, they too, disappeared. There was nothing as far as we could see. The sea was calm. The ship's engines churned the water as they pushed the vessel forward, leaving behind a white water wave. We forgot time as we stood at the railing mesmerized by this show.

"Which will be the first port we'll come to?" I asked. I knew it was in northern Spain but had forgotten the name.

"We will anchor in Santander and then in La Coruña," Dad answered. After that we will be in the open sea until we reach the Caribbean. It should not take more than a week to ten days."

We began to explore the ship. One important location we had found already before, and that was the bathroom. And having found it, we also discovered that we had to remember our first Spanish word: *ocupado* (occupied).

Now it was important to locate the dining room. Our stomach was reminding us that we hadn't eaten anything since breakfast. Besides, the schedule, which we were given at boarding, indicated that dinner would be served in thirty minutes. We found a dining room nicely decorated with round tables and comfortable chairs. To our dismay, we were not seated. We were told in no uncertain terms that this was for first-and second-class passengers only, and that we were to go further down the hallway, where we would find another dining room. Well, what a difference! We had rectangular tables with benches on both sides, picknick style. It looked like a pizza joint!

But no matter the furnishings, we found a nice group of people to sit and have our meals with. We actually had a lot of fun. And, who knows, maybe even more so than the "stuffed shirts" in first class.

During the next few days it was interesting to watch all the ship's maneuverings as we anchored in Santander and La Coruña. Spaniards came on board, filling the rest of the vacant cabins. Smaller boats brought their luggage and big travel chests. Other boats ferried over a variety of crates, barrels and sacks, probably supplies and groceries needed for the long crossing of the Atlantic.

We went on land for a few hours to take a look at the city and people and go window-shopping. A small boat brought us back to the side of the ship, where we had to climb up the not-too-steady stairs. Once all passengers were on board and accounted for, the hanging stairs were pulled up and fastened on the side of the ship.

During the following days, there was not much else to do but look at the ocean and the sky, observe a few flying fish and many schools of dolphins. They seemed to enjoy themselves swimming alongside the ship. Their shiny bodies glistened in the sunshine when they jumped out of the water. In the late afternoons, people gathered on deck to watch the sunsets.

For three days we had bad weather. Even though the *Reina del Pacifico* was a big ship, we could distinctively feel the ups and downs of the waves. It made walking along the hallways somewhat difficult. We stubbed our feet on the floor with the upward motion and seemed to jump forward with the downward one. The dining room was frequented less and less. Seasickness had taken over. The one lady in our cabin never left her cot from the beginning of the trip to the very end. Luckily we were not affected by this dreadfulness.

"Look, Mom, I can see seagulls. We must be getting close to land," I called out one day.

"We must be approaching the Bermuda Islands," Dad commented, looking at the itinerary he had brought from the cabin. And, indeed, later on we saw many small islands with lush tropical vegetation, but most of them seemed to be uninhabited.

After spending a few hours in Bermuda, the ship continued on. Not in every port could we go on land, but there was always much to see from the deck. The hustle and bustle down below on the pier, cranes lifting big bundles and crates from one place to another, people shouting out orders, and men unloading trucks carrying the heavy sacks on their bare shoulders. It was a picture of constant motion.

The outside temperature was getting warmer. The water was not so grayish blue anymore either, but turning a lighter blue with some turquoise and green in it. It was much clearer. It had definitely a tropical feeling to it.

One day, sailors set up a very primitive swimming pool on deck. It was something like a giant rectangular canvas bag filled with water. We kids didn't mind at all. Water was water, no matter the container.

We arrived at our next destination, which was Nassau in the Bahamas. By now the ocean had become almost transparent. Meanwhile the ship was busy loading and unloading, young black boys and men, sitting in small boats, entertained us. Passengers along the railing threw silvery coins into the water and the boys dove after them, retrieving every single one. Copper-colored coins were of no interest. Maybe they could not be easily seen in the water or just were not worth the effort.

The following port of call was Havana followed by Kingston, Jamaica. Passengers wanting to go on land in Kingston were warned by the captain to stay on the main road and not to venture into side streets. He said that muggers were everywhere. From what we saw, it must have been true. On every street corner there stood a policeman. We walked along the main avenue past the governor's mansion behind big wrought iron gates and then turned back. It felt good to be on firm land again.

From there we sailed to Cartagena, a Colombian port, and Cristobal Colon, Panama.

Going through the Panama Canal was very impressive. Upon entering the canal, a canal pilot came on board and took complete charge of the ship. It is about seven miles to the locks, which consist of three chambers. Small electric locomotives on both sides of the locks pulled the ship forward. The locomotives ran up an incline at the end of each chamber to reach the next higher level. This allowed the same set of locomotives to pull vessels through all three locks. The ships are lifted about 85 feet from sea level. From there the vessels continue under their own power for about 22 miles crossing Lake Gatun, which was formed by damming a river. At the end of Lake Gatun ships enter the 8-mile long, 500 feet wide man-made channel or cut, which leads to another set of three locks, which will lower the ships back to sea level. It takes about eight hours to travel from the Atlantic to the Pacific.

Upon leaving Panama, we sailed down the west coast of South America, passing Colombia and Ecuador. The seawater had changed back to the grayish blue color of the Atlantic even though now we were sailing the Pacific Ocean. We ate our first avocados and chirimoyas. At that time the avocados did not impress us. The chirimoyas, on the other hand, were delicious. They have a very unique sweet flavor hard to describe. It is a very delicate fruit that bruises easily. In Callao, Peru, we went on land, accompanying a German lady to her final destination in Lima. We visited for a while and then returned to the ship. Our voyage hadn't ended yet.

The next stop was Arica, the northernmost port of Chile. Then came Antofagasta and, finally, Valparaiso. We had made it. We had been on the *Reina del Pacifico* for four weeks. It was May 20, 1949, the beginning of a new chapter in our lives.

Reina del Pacifico traversing the Panama canal.

THE PACIFIC STEAM NAVIGATION COMPANY

PACIFIC BUILDING · JAMES STREET · LIVERPOOL·2

ROUND VOYAGES

via BERMUDA · NASSAU · HAVANA
JAMAICA & PANAMA CANAL *to*
WEST COAST *of* SOUTH AMERICA

m.v. "Reina del Pacifico"

SAILINGS DURING 1955

Outward

LIVERPOOL	14 Jany.	5 April	23 June	13 Sept.	27 Oct.
LA ROCHELLE - PALLICE	16 ,,	7 ,,	25 ,,	15 ,,	29 ,,
SANTANDER	17 ,,	8 ,,	26 ,,	16 ,,	30 ,,
CORUNA	18 ,,	9 ,,	27 ,,	17 ,,	31 ,,
BERMUDA	25 ,,	16 ,,	4 July	24 5 ,,	7 Nov.
NASSAU	27 ,,	18 ,,	6 ,,	27 ,,	9 ,,
HAVANA	28 9 ,,	19 20 ,,	7 8 ,,	28 9 ,,	10 11 ,,
KINGSTON	31 ,,	22 ,,	10 ,,	1 Oct	13 ,,
CARTAGENA	2 Feby.	24 ,,	12 ,,		15 ,,
CRISTOBAL (Panama Canal)	3 ,,	25 ,,	13 ,,		16 ,,
LA LIBERTAD	5 ,,	27 ,,	15 ,,		18 ,,
CALLAO	7 8 ,,	29 30 ,,	17 18 ,,		20 21 ,,
ARICA	10 ,,	2 May	20 ,,		23 ,,
MEJILLONES	11 ,,	3 ,,	21 ,,		24 ,,
ANTOFAGASTA	11 ,,	3 ,,	21 ,,		24 ,,
VALPARAISO	13 ,,	5 ,,	23 ,,		26 ,,

SHIP WILL NOT NECESSARILY REMAIN AT VALPARAISO DURING THE
TURN ROUND BUT MAY PROCEED TO SAN ANTONIO OR OTHER
CHILEAN PORT FOR HOMEWARD LOADING.

Homeward

VALPARAISO	17 Feby.	9 May	27 July		10 Nov.
ANTOFAGASTA	19 ,,	11 ,,	29 ,,		2 Dec.
MEJILLONES	19 ,,	11 ,,	29 ,,		2 ,,
MOLLENDO (if calling)	20 ,,	12 ,,	30 ,,		3 ,,
*CALLAO	22 ,,	14 ,,	1 Aug.		5 ,,
LA LIBERTAD	24 ,,	17 ,,	4 ,,		8 ,,
CRISTOBAL (Panama Canal)	26 7 ,,	19 ,,	6 ,,		10 ,,
CARTAGENA	23 ,,	20 ,,	7 ,,		11 ,,
KINGSTON		22 ,,	9 ,,	2 Oct	13 ,,
HAVANA	3 4 Mar.	24 5 ,,	11 12 ,,	4 ,,	15 16 ,,
NASSAU	5 ,,	26 ,,	13 ,,		17 ,,
BERMUDA	7 8 ,,	28 ,,	15 ,,	7 8 ,,	19 ,,
CORUNA	15 ,,	4 June	22 ,,	15 ,,	26 ,,
SANTANDER	16 ,,	5 ,,	23 ,,		27 ,,
LA ROCHELLE - PALLICE	17 ,,	6 ,,	24 ,,		28 ,,
PLYMOUTH	18 ,,	7 ,,	25 ,,		29 ,,
LIVERPOOL	19 ,,	8 ,,	26 ,,	17 ,,	30 ,,

*Provisional dates only, being dependent on Homeward loading programme arranged on the Peruvian Coast.

SAILINGS ARE SUBJECT TO ALTERATION AND/OR CANCELLATION
WITHOUT PREVIOUS NOTICE.

PASSENGER DEPARTMENT,
November, 1954

South America

A NEW BEGINNING

So this was Valparaiso. Up to the days the Panama Canal was built, it was the port to come to. After having sailed around treacherous Cape Horn and through the rough and dangerous waters of the Strait of Magellan where many ships litter the ocean floor, captains anchored their ships with much relief in Valparaiso's harbor. They replenished their food and fresh water supplies, obtained whatever else was needed, and gave their shipmen needed rest.

Gold-rush people, not wanting to go on a wagon trail to California, came through on their way to San Francisco. Commerce and trade flourished. Chile was the main exporter of Saltpeter or nitrate, in its natural state. It was used as agricultural fertilizer and in the manufacture of gunpowder and therefore much in demand. Large copper deposits were mined in the north of Chile. Quickly Valparaiso became the second largest city in Chile.

And here we were now, getting closer to the harbor. From the distance we could see the town built against the foothills of the coastal mountain range. Coming closer, we were able to distinguish big buildings, which seemed to house the harbor authorities. The Reina Del Pacifico was slowing down. We could see figures on the pier. Soon they transformed into people with faces. One of those had to be my uncle I had never seen. The ship turned sideways parallel to the pier. Engines set into reverse brought her to a complete stop. Anchors dropped into the water. Next the gangway was put in place and the hustle and bustle began.

Seemingly, all the passengers were on deck waiting for a word from the captain allowing them to disembark. We stood at the railing sandwiched between other people. Mom was looking for her brother. Would she recognize him after all those years? The last time she saw him, was in early 1927, when he left Germany after completing his studies at the university. Now he was a 48-year-old widower.

"I see him, I see him. There he is," she called out suddenly, pointing to a figure on the pier. "I am sure it is my brother. I am positive!" Mom kept saying.

It took us all afternoon to disembark, do the paperwork, go through customs and get settled in a hotel a few blocks away. And yes, Mom was right. It was her brother she had seen from the deck of the ship.

Uncle Curt was close to six feet tall and weighed about 180 pounds. He had brown eyes and his light brown hair was parted on the side. His thin-lipped mouth was set back more than usual between his long nose and forward curving chin. He told me one time later on that it was difficult for him to eat an ice cream cone without getting ice cream on his nose.

We stayed up late that evening, talking and talking, getting acquainted and re-acquainted again. That evening was also had an introduction to local customs: dinnertime was not until around 10:00 at night, way past my bedtime. And another strange thing I saw: most diners were not finishing their food, leaving quite a bit of it on their plates. What a waste! Why did they do that? Uncle Curt explained that they did not want to seem to be starving. Another custom we had to get used to as hard as it was.

The next day was May 21st, an important holiday in Chile commemorating a sea battle between Chile and Peru in 1879. From the window of our hotel we had an excellent view of the marching band and the military parade that followed. The cadets from the Chilean Naval Academy looked very handsome in their white parade uniforms. Flags and decorations were everywhere.

"Listen," we said almost in unison, "they are playing "Erika" our German march." What excitement on this first day! Was that an omen of good things to come?

After lunch we all climbed into my uncle's car and started the last segment of our trip. Santiago, the capital of Chile, is about 85 miles east of Valparaiso. We had to cross the coastal mountain range on a curvy two-lane road, climbing up to about 2,000 feet. Just before we got to the summit, my uncle stopped the car, saying that he wanted to show us something. There was not much to see. On one side of the road the mountain continued upwards, and next to the other side a big boulder protruded from the ground and several hundred feet below one could see a small river.

"This boulder here saved my life yesterday!" my uncle said. "It had been raining, the road was slick and after the curve my car spun around. When I came to a standstill, the back of my car was sitting on that boulder!"

We could see how upset he was getting just by visualizing it again. When we got closer to Santiago, we stopped at what seemed to be a small shrine by the side of the road. My uncle put some money into the box and then proceeded to tell us that this saint was thought of as a protector of all travelers. Many times in years to come I saw people stop there to ask for blessings for a trip to be embarked on or to give thanks for having come home safely.

We passed several clusters of small houses along the sides of the road. Streetwise skinny dogs ran around looking for scraps of food. Small children played in the dirt under the watchful eyes of their grandmothers. All seemed very quiet and tranquil; it was siesta time. Small fields were planted in corn and each house, no matter how small, had one of those typical Chilean grape arbors one could sit under on hot summer days.

Soon we reached the outskirts of Santiago, a city then of about three million people. Many streets were decorated with red-white and blue banners, the national colors. Trolleybuses, taxis and private cars carried small flags. It was definitely a festive atmosphere.

My uncle lived on the other side of Santiago, closer to the Andes Mountains. This gave us a chance to see more of the city as we traveled through on the main boulevard Alameda. We came by the Chilean White House, la Moneda, with honor guards on both sides of the entrance and a big monument in front depicting one of the past presidents. About ten blocks down the street was Cerro Santa Lucía, a small mountain within the city made into a park with many benches, decorative fountains and exotic trees. Then we drove along the Mapocho River, which runs through parts of the city, and finally my uncle turned into a driveway. We had arrived.

It was a big white two-story house with a flat roof and very modern in style. The front yard consisted of a small lawn surrounded by bushes and flowers, and a wrought iron fence separated it from the street. In the back of the house was a patio with a couple of shade trees and the cloth lines. Laundry was all done by hand then and hung up to dry.

People emerged from the house urging us to come inside. Mom and Dad were taken to a bedroom upstairs and I had my own little room downstairs. What luxury! After we had unloaded the car and freshened up a bit, we gathered in the living room. My uncle explained that these were the two sisters of his deceased wife and that they were running the household for him. They both lived there, one with her husband and a little four-year-old boy. And they all spoke only Spanish, with the exception of my uncle. We had to do some fast learning!

At 4:30 the table was set. It was teatime. I will always remember that almost boiling tea, so strong that it looked like coffee. Most of the time I was the last one to finish my meal. Sandwiches and cake were served and everybody ate. There was more talk until ten o'clock when dinner was ready: salad, soup, main dish and dessert. I was so tired but I made it through, and so ended our first day in a new country.

INDEPENDENCE

It was the year 1950. We were still living with my uncle Curt, blending into the household as best as we could. Actually we didn't have to do very much, just keep our rooms in order. A live-in maid did the cleaning and the cooking.

I think my uncle liked having us around. He had been a widower now for five years, didn't have any children, and was lonely. He was an avid reader of biographies and history books. Reading was good, a live conversation sometimes better. He could talk now about old times with my mom and dad. Friends and relatives came alive again in his memory, people from his youth. He learned of their lives, their whereabouts and of some of their deaths in the war. There was so much to tell. The family had been separated for so many years.

Uncle Curt was an engineer by profession. He was working in a company specializing in heating and air conditioning. He liked his job and was good at it. But he also had another passion and that was his music. He played the cello. He was a tall man and the cello fit his size. Once a month three other friends came to the house and they made beautiful music. The quartet was composed of cello, two violins and a viola. They played with such enthusiasm and concentration that often time was forgotten.

By getting together with these musician-friends, he kept up a tradition from his parents and grandparents homes. Music was very much appreciated there and everybody played an instrument or sang. It was a welcome form of entertainment.

When he was not playing the cello, he listened to classical music on the old 78 and 33 rpm records. Many times he turned the volume up so high we could hear it throughout the house. His argument was, that that was the way it sounded in the concert hall. I had a few favorites among his records and sometimes played them after school. I loved to listen to Marion Anderson with her great contralto voice. She was to become the first black female singer to perform at the Metropolitan Opera and was invited to sing at the inauguration of President John F. Kennedy.

"Would you like to play the cello?" my uncle asked me one day, "I'll give you one of mine if you want to learn." I didn't want to hurt his feelings but at the same time had to be honest.

"No thank you, but thanks for the offer," I replied. Had it been another instrument, maybe my answer would have been different, but a cello? No.

Dad had started a business with one of my uncle's German-and Spanish-speaking friends repairing and building all kinds of electronic equipment.

Mom got a job in a photography shop. I still don't know how she managed to communicate with customers. I guess a few words, a smile and sign language go a long way.

Sometimes Mom and I went window-shopping and also people watching. Everything was new to us and interesting. Women dressed very well, wore high heels and make-up. Earrings and other jewelry gave the final touch. No wonder men whistled when they walked by. That type of compliment was new to us too, but we learned to appreciate it. It was fun. Men were very courteous toward women. When walking on a sidewalk with a lady they always were between her and the street, protecting her from danger. The Don Juan spirit, the Latin blood was very much noticeable.

Businesses and stores were open from eight to noon and from four to eight Monday through Friday and eight to one on Saturdays. The majority of workers went home for lunch and came back for the second half. It produced a constant rush hour. Buses were filled to the brim. People were packed in the aisles and hanging out the doors by standing on the steps and holding on for dear life.

One day I came home from school and saw that everybody was very excited about something.

"What is going on, what is happening?" I asked.

"That's right, you don't know yet. We received good news today," my uncle said. "Your Aunt Rita and Uncle Harry have all their permits and visas and will be here in six weeks." His face was beaming with happiness as he was telling me this. He was walking about the living room, too animated to sit still.

This was good news, indeed. I loved my aunt Rita, Mom's sister. She was a vivacious person who loved to laugh. She was outspoken and hard working. Horses were her passion. But she was also no stranger to great heartache and sorrow. Her only child, a seventeen-year-old son, was drafted during the last couple of months of WW II, sent to the Russian front and was never seen again. Searches by the Red Cross as to his whereabouts were fruitless. It would be good for her to see her brother again after 23 years. Now the whole family would be together once more.

The day of their arrival came quickly. My uncle's sister–in-law and her family, living with him, had bought a house and moved out a few weeks prior. Now there was room for the newcomers. I listened to the conversations of times past. There was talk about the times of WW I, and how hard it was to just stay alive. Food was scarce and personal security nonexistent. They were children then, but had not forgotten much. They reminisced about their childhood, people they knew, specific events and family gatherings. WW II was talked about and how it all affected us.

I just remember one of the stories. It was during the Russian occupation at the end of WW I, when a friend or relative was ill, unable to get out of bed. He was in a downstairs bedroom. A large group of Russian soldiers stormed into the house looking for men to take prisoner. They leaned their rifles against the wall and adjacent door and, with pistols in hand, ran through the house searching each room, the attic and cellar. When they could not find anybody, they took their rifles and left. The only room they did not search was the one they had leaned their rifles on and that was the room that person was in.

It was a life saving break for the ill man, for prisoners usually landed in forced labor camps in Siberia never to return again.

Uncle Harry was an agronomist and soon found a job on a dairy farm close to Santiago. It was not a great job, but a beginning, and they were happy. We visited them quite often. It was good to see them, to get out of the big city, and breathe clean country air. To this day the smell of freshly cut alfalfa or grass for that matter and the odors of a cow barn or horse stable remind me of happy and carefree times.

The following year he was offered the management of a big farm in the south of Chile. From then on I spent all my summer vacations there.

In the meantime another family had arrived from Germany. They were the parents and sister of a lady, who came to Chile a year earlier and lived close by. She had previously approached my uncle for financial help in covering their travel expenses to Chile. They too were originally from Estonia.

My uncle took a fancy to this newly arrived sister. She was twenty-six years his junior, but that didn't seem to matter. A few months later, they got engaged. They were married almost 50 years and had three children. He died suddenly in 2001 at ninety-nine years of age, having stopped working just two years before. He was employed by the same company for seventy years, working first for the owner of the firm and later for his son!

Mom, Dad and I stayed with my uncle for about one year and then moved into a one-bedroom rented apartment. It was the first time since we left Estonia in 1939 that we had our own place, our own kitchen, and our own bathroom. We didn't have to share anything with anybody. It was a wonderful feeling.

After so many years we were finally independent.

MY LAST SCHOOL YEARS

"It is time for you to go back to school!" my mother said one day at the beginning of June of 1949. We had been in Chile now for about two weeks getting acquainted with our new surroundings.

Chile has a very large German population, especially in Santiago and in the southern cities of Valdivia, Osorno and Puerto Montt. Many of those immigrants came as early as the 1850's. They worked the land, were proficient in their trades and became well-respected citizens. German schools sprang up in all of those towns. Santiago had and still has a German hospital, church, a private sports club, restaurants and its own weekly newspaper.

I was accepted at a German school about a mile away from my uncle's house. It was a gray, three-story u-shaped building. It looked very stern and business-like, not inviting at all. In the center of the school was a small schoolyard with a few shade trees. Adjacent to it was a basketball court, and to the side a small playground for younger students. In the back, behind the basketball court, stood a little one-story, one-room house. Youth groups had their meetings there and practiced German folk dances, among other things.

The principal was a man in his late forties, just as stern-looking as the school building. He was slender and walked erect in his double-breasted dark suit. His slick dark hair was parted in the middle, showing the white line of his scalp. Two curly waves on each side were combed back, matching each other. They never moved. Dark-rimmed glasses adorned his nose, and his cheeks were sunken. He was soft-spoken, but after our initial visit, I never talked to him again.

I was placed in the equivalent of eighth grade. From first grade to the sixth, classes were taught in German. It was a condition of acceptance to be fluent in German. Starting with the seventh grade to the twelfth, all classes were taught in Spanish. The reason for that was that students in foreign private schools were tested by Chilean teachers at the end of each of the last six school years.

The school year had commenced at the beginning of March. Right from the start, I was behind. I listened to the teachers, but didn't understand a word they were saying. I tried to write down what I heard. Gradually I learned, but it wasn't easy. At the end of ninth grade, I was tested in all three grades, seventh to ninth. Apparently I did not learn enough. I passed two, but failed ninth grade.

It was then that I decided to go to a Chilean school for a year to do ninth grade over again. I had to get away from hearing so much German. It turned out to be a good idea. At the end of the year, I passed easily. The following year I returned to the German school and all was well. I enjoyed school, made friends and participated in school outings.

"Would you like to go skiing during winter break?" my girlfriend Imme asked one day. "A list is circulating and we could sign up. It is not expensive." Of course, I wanted to go, and after getting my parents approval, I signed up.

We had to take everything we needed for a week's stay: clothing, food, a one-burner camping stove, a small pot to cook in, a flashlight, etc. Nothing was supplied at the cabin but the roof over our heads. All had to fit into the backpack, with the sleeping bag on top. It was not an easy task. By the time the departure day came, I had packed and repacked several times.

Early one morning a truck came to the school to pick us up. There were enough benches in the back for the group to sit on, with room to spare for backpacks and skis. It was cold, but we were too excited to notice. Once we were out of the city and in the foothills of the Andes, the road became so narrow that two cars could not pass each other. The unwritten rule was: up the mountain in the morning and down after 1:00 PM. It was the only road to Farellones, a little village further up, consisting of cabins belonging to ski enthusiasts and one restaurant.

It didn't take very long, maybe an hour, to get to the point where the truck dropped us off. Mules and their handlers were waiting for us. The animals stood there dozing in the early sunshine with their tails in constant motion swishing away pesky flies. The sun was just now peeking over the mountains, bringing life to nature. Birds were awakening and ground squirrels looked at us from a safe distance.

Before loading the backpacks and skis on the mules, they had to be blindfolded. Mules are smart. They don't like to carry heavy cargo and become difficult to handle by not standing still. Once all was loaded and blindfolds removed, they started the march into the canyon and up the mountain urged on by the guides. There was no road, just a trail. The snow level was at a higher altitude and therefore it was easy walking uphill. We were all in good spirits, laughing and joking, overflowing with energy as we followed the mules. We kept up pretty well. But as time went by, the line of climbers became longer and longer and laughter less frequent. We were all breathing hard, as we were now walking through snow.

It took an average of five hours for everybody to reach the primitive stone cabin. The two-feet-high snow on the roof had been pushed down, uncovering the metal sheeting. Long heavy icicles hung from the edges of the roof, glistening in the light. They, too, had to be knocked off, for they could hurt somebody were they to fall down. The cabin was just big enough to house us and our supervisors and chaperones, a married couple sent along by the school. The main room had a big potbelly stove in the middle and several picnic tables with benches along two walls. Adjacent to this room were two bedrooms, one for the girls and one for the boys. There were no beds, just a big platform, where about six to seven people could sleep next to each other, and a large second story above it, bunk-bed style, for another group. Both were covered with fresh-smelling straw for cushioning and warmth. The couple in charge of us had a tiny room to themselves.

There was no kitchen, no bathroom, no running water, and no electricity in the cabin. An outhouse was placed strategically over a steep cliff. We always hoped for no wind and updraft when using it. Water could be obtained from a basin filled by a spring, which collected there and overflowed to disappear down the mountain. One freezing night it had snowed heavily. Most of the basin had a layer of ice on it and was totally covered with snow. Needless to say, we barely brushed our teeth.

Skiing was fun, even though we had no ski lifts to take us up the slopes. Once, some of us ventured cross-country to the next mountain. The view was beautiful in every direction, the glistening white snow untouched, and the silence complete.

I could hear only my pumping heart and the sound of the skis in the powdery snow, as I followed the single line of friends ahead of me. It was almost dark when we returned to our cabin. For me this outing was an accomplishment I was proud of, since I was just learning to ski.

The days went by quickly. We skied, played games, sang songs, accompanied by an accordion one of the students had brought, or just sunbathed. Before long, our supply of clean clothes was coming to an end. Food reserves also became precariously low. We barely made it to the last day, when all leftovers were shared and consumed.

Finally, the mules came, were loaded and we went back to civilization. A wonderful week in the mountains was over, but the memories stayed.

School and homework took up most of my time.

Sometimes the whole family went to the movies, which was a special affair. Tickets were bought in advance with assigned seating. We dressed up for the occasion. Before the show, we splurged with a visit to a café where the pastries were heavenly. From there we walked over to the nearby theater. An usher seated us, for which he got tipped. The movie theater was decorated beautifully. Large candelabras hung from the ceiling, velvet drapes decorated the doors and walls, and the large curtain over the screen was like a promise of good things to come.

First we watched the latest world news: Konrad Adenauer became Chancellor of West Germany, Rodgers and Hammerstein produced the show *South Pacific*, and the first bikinis came under scrutiny. The intermission was the last chance for latecomers to get seated and then the show started. Candies had to stay in their wrappers and no more talking was allowed.

Movies were in English with Spanish subtitles, but that didn't present a problem for me anymore. I had learned the language.

1953 - I am in the front row, second from the left

Transfer from truck to mules

A long 5 hour climb up to the cabin

Our home for a week

Rhona second from right

On the top of the mountain

Early morning clean-up at the only source of water

A TRIP TO LLIFEN

In Chile the school year ends mid-December, and summer recess lasts until mid- March. It was the year 1952. I had taken my sophomore exams and was done for the year. A few days after New Year, I told my parents, "I would like to visit Aunt Rita!" She and my uncle lived in the south of Chile, where he was the administrator of a big "fundo," or farm.

"Of course you can, but we have to find out if there are still tickets available for the "Nocturno," my mother answered.

The "Nocturno" was the well-known nightly train, with a diner and several sleeper wagons among others, but by no means an Orient Express. It was still early in January, and most vacationers leave in February to their vacation spots, so I was lucky to get a seat in the sleeper section of the train.

My parents took me to the central train station in Santiago where at 6 PM the "Nocturno" would depart. The porter took my suitcase and brought it to my seat. Mom and Dad said good-bye and left. I was on my own and ready for the adventure.

The conductor waved to the porters and attendants that it was time to leave. Whistles blew, latecomers came running and shouting, but the doors finally closed. The locomotive began to release some steam and I heard sounds of metal banging against metal, as the wagons slowly started to move. Finally we were in the open leaving the station behind.

I settled into my seat, knowing that this would be my home for the next 15 hours. About 15 minutes into the journey, a polite uniformed man came to check the tickets and offer some magazines.

"Dinner will be ready at 7:30. Would you like to make a reservation?" he asked. I declined, because Mom had prepared a big bag of sandwiches and fruit for me.

By 9:00 PM the sun had set and it was getting dark. A crew of workers began to make the beds by flattening the two opposite seats for the lower bunk, and for the upper one they unfolded a platform that had been fastened to the wall. Both beds had fresh linens, warm blankets, fluffy pillows and a small night light, bright enough to permit reading. Finally drapes were unfolded for privacy. We had paid for the lower bunk, which was nicer. It had the window to look out, and it was easier to get in. The upper bunk required using a ladder. At 10:00 the lights in the hallway were dimmed and all was quiet. At 7:00 the next morning everybody was up and the "bedroom" was again transformed into a normal train, with everybody anxious to get to his or her destination. After a couple of hours we were in La Union, where I got off. This was the first leg of the trip, soon we would be off to the second one.

"Where and when does the next train to Lago Ranco leave?" I asked an uniformed man behind a little window.

"Well, señorita, that one should be here in about 30 minutes, you'll have enough time for a cup of coffee across the street at Dona Maria's and then come back to this same platform."

I bought my ticket and waited. 30 minutes turned into 40 and this small commuter train was nowhere to be seen. When it finally arrived after almost an hour, it was quite full but I found a seat next to an open window. Great, I could see out! Whistles blew, doors closed and we were on our way. As the train gained speed and air mixed with some smoke came in through the window, it became clear to me why this seat was available: the window was stuck and could not be closed! So I took my suitcase, put it in the aisle and sat on it the rest of the way.

Two hours later, I saw the beautiful Lake Ranco. It was big, more like a small ocean; a couple of islands were visible, some small boats in the distance and the opposite shore too far to distinguish. I had to get to that shore to a little village called Llifen!

I walked to the landing of the ferry and saw a boat already loaded with all sorts of crates, barrels, sacks, cages with animals, and people with their big ponchos sitting along the railing or standing. The captain was waiting for the newcomers from the train. We were late in arriving, so they were late in leaving, but nobody complained. It was the only way to get across the lake. I paid my fare and found a spot where I could sit on my suitcase again.

"Buenos dias, señorita. Where are you going?" asked the captain. He could tell I was not from the area. I stuck out like a sore thumb with my blond hair.

"Have to go to Llifen and then on to the fundo Santa Juana," I answered.

"Oh yes, I know Don Harry and la señora Rita. Do they know you are coming?"

"No, it is a surprise."

"Well, then you have to catch the milk truck. Haven't seen any other vehicle come down to Llifen this morning. Maybe we will make it in time for you to get a ride."

I knew about the milk truck. It made this trip every day up the one and only road for about ten miles to fetch the milk from the dairies. Santa Juana was only six miles away, well within the distance for me to borrow a horse and ride it if needed. I was well prepared, wearing jeans and high top-shoes, and my suitcase was not big or heavy. The horse, I knew, I could borrow at the small restaurant whose owners were acquainted with my aunt and uncle.

In the meantime I just enjoyed the boat ride, hoped for the best and ate the rest of my food. The sun was shining, it was warm, and no wind had come up. One could only hear the water splash against the sides of the boat and the monotonous humming of the engines. Conversation became sparse as many travelers allowed themselves to take a little siesta. Once in a while, a fish jumped out of the water and fell back in, causing circles to form on the surface. We passed the two islands and others behind those. Just now one could see land in the far distance, or was it a cloud?

After 2 ½ hours we arrived in Llifen. By now it was close to 3:30 in the afternoon. Everybody scrambled out of the boat and the unloading began. I went over to where the milk truck should be parked before it started on its route. I was lucky and so were other people, who also wanted to hitch a ride. Since there were no buses in that area or other modes of transportation except on horseback or on foot, it almost became an unwritten rule that one would wait for the connecting train and boat. We all got on the back of the truck, sat on the large milk cans, and made sure we had something to hold on to. The road was just dirt and gravel, full of holes and washed out in many places by the winter rains. Things don't get repaired quickly in that part of the country, maybe not even until the following year. After a short while, the driver stopped in front of Aunt Rita's gate. I gave him a good tip, waved good-bye to the others, and walked toward the house. Finally I had arrived.

It took almost 24 hours to travel less than 700 miles.

"Hallo, somebody home? Aunt Rita, are you here?" I called out as I entered the back door. Dead silence, like nobody lived in the place. I left my suitcase in the kitchen and went outside toward the barn. It was milking time and somebody had to be there. The cows were all in place chomping their fresh clover. Once in a while, I could hear the metal sound of a milk bucket. Maybe the cow had moved and the bucket had to be adjusted. Milking was done the old-fashioned way: by hand sitting on a small stool holding the bucket between the knees. The air was heavy and humid. It smelled definitely like "country," but that was good; I loved it.

"Señorita, can I help you? Are you looking for someone?" a voice behind me called out. I turned around and faced a man standing there with a bucket full of warm milk.

"Yes, I am looking for Señora Rita or Don Harry. Do you know where they are?"

"Bueno, they went to the pasture up the road," he replied.

"Gracias, I will wait at the house," I said as I watched him pour the milk into a big metal can to be picked up by the milk truck the following morning.

The house was a wooden structure built against a steep slope. From the front it looked like a one-story house with a tin roof and a veranda going all the way around. On the opposite side though one could see another floor below with windows facing the back. There was no electricity in the house, no telephone. The kitchen had running water by way of gravity. A pipe was connected to a tank on a near-by mountain. This tank was fed by a small stream. The outhouse was in the back, hidden by some bushes, but one could not miss it because of the well-worn path leading to it.

The house was primitive by today's standards, but cozy. I loved the big fireplace in the living room with thick sheepskins in front of it. Nothing was better than sitting there with a good book. Sometimes the burning logs radiated so much heat that I had to move back. Leaning against the couch, I watched the flames and listened to the sounds of the burning wood. Some logs were wet. As they heated up, moisture came out at the ends, making a hissing sound. Lumps of sap burned like sparklers and occasionally one could here a loud bang.

Did I hear something? Yes, someone had come into the kitchen. I opened the door to check. Immediately a dog started to bark at me. My aunt spun around and for a few moments was speechless.

"Harry, Harry, come quick, we have company. You will never guess who is here!" she cried out.

"What's all the commotion?" said Uncle Harry as he walked in. Then he saw me. "Well, well, what do you know? Why didn't you let us know you were coming? We could have picked you up in Llifen."

The dog stopped barking. He realized that I was not an intruder. My aunt and uncle removed their riding boots and we went into the living room. I had to answer hundreds of questions, tell all the details of my uncle's life in Santiago and ours, and every little gossip. News got to them very infrequently. Our family was not good at maintaining a lively correspondence and there was no phone. We talked until it got dark and the kerosene lamp had to be lit. We had dinner, talked some more and finally went to bed. It had been a long day for all three of us.

My room was in the attic. The walls, floor and ceiling were all wood. The room was small. It was furnished with a bed, a small stand for a big bowl and a jug of water to wash-up and a chamber pot under the bed. No nightstand, no chair. Many nails on the wall, which served as hangers, replaced the dresser. But the mattress was wonderful! So soft and warm! These mattresses were all hand made, stuffed with wool. Every three to four years, or when needed, they were taken apart. The wool was washed, fluffed up and then the mattresses were re-stuffed. Mattresses like that last forever.

The next morning I was awakened by the smell of freshly baked bread. Juanita, the good fairy of the house who was in charge of cleaning and cooking, had been busy this morning. I went downstairs and found my aunt still at the breakfast table. Uncle Harry had already left on his rounds. It was a large farm and required constant attention. I ate quickly. We wanted to ride to a neighboring farm, say hello and invite them for dinner next Sunday.

"Juan, please get my horse and Cognac for la señorita," my aunt called out to a man working close to the stable. Cognac was to be my horse for the duration of my stay. The man took a harness and went over to the corral to get my aunt's horse. Mine was in a pasture and had to be lassoed. In the meantime, I went to the kitchen to fetch a couple of apples for Cognac. We quickly became friends. After two weeks, I just had to call him and he trotted over to where I was to collect his prize. I didn't depend on Juan anymore.

It was a nice coincidence that today water was being heated in the kitchen. It was bath day! Just what I needed for my sore muscles to relax. The fire in the stove was going strong. The stovetop actually got red. The tub was in a small bathroom next to the kitchen. I didn't mind then that my turn came after my uncle and aunt had stepped into that tub to take their baths. We just added another pot of boiling water to make it warmer again. Yes, that's right, we all three took a bath in the same water!

After a few days, I had blended into the daily routine of farm life. Uncle Harry tended to the fields and Aunt Rita was in charge of the animals. She loved horses more than anything and was an excellent rider. She became well known and respected in "horse circles" and many people consulted her expertise before buying an expensive animal. Later on she was a judge in various equestrian events.

Weeks went by quickly. On weekends we visited neighbors or they came to see us. Card games were played, mostly Bridge and Canasta. Once, my aunt organized a fox hunt. She was the fox and rode off with a ten-minute head start. She pinned visible written messages on trees with clues to where to ride next. It took us forever to find her, but it was a lot of fun.

By now it was February. Harvest time was upon us. Equipment was checked and preparations were made. It was busy time for everybody. Those were the last days of my stay in Santa Juana. In March school started again and I had to return to Santiago. But saying goodbye was not hard. I knew I was coming back next year.

Cognac, my mode of transportation and
Marulli, my daily companion

A DAY IN THE COUNTRY

It was summertime in the south of Chile where I was spending a couple of months with Aunt Rita, my mother's sister, and her husband Uncle Harry. He was overseeing a good-sized farm located close to the foothills of the Andes Mountains. They shared some of the responsibilities. Uncle Harry dedicated himself to the care of the fields and pastures, the clearing of additional land from trees and stumps, and Aunt Rita minded the animals: a small herd of horses, about twenty cows, pigs, and some sheep, goats, and chickens.

I loved life in the country. It was such a big contrast to the hustle and bustle of the city with its noisy cars and blasting horns. The multitude of serious looking people all in a hurry to get to wherever they were going. Buses filled to capacity with bodies, squeezed into seats and the ones standing in the aisles compacted into a big mass holding on to the bars overhead.

I preferred the outdoors, the clear and unpolluted air. I liked the peaceful silence interrupted only by chirping birds, barking dogs, and the occasional car or truck coming by with friendly drivers who smiled and waived. I liked to take walks with Marulli, a dog that adopted and followed me wherever I went wether I was on foot or on horseback.

I visited my aunt and uncle during school vacations. Being with them didn't entitle me though to laziness and loafing around, however. I had to work and participate in the daily activities. Earn my keep so to say but I did not mind at all.

"Rhona, you have to help me out today," Aunt Rita said one day early in the morning as she pulled on her well worn brown riding boots. "I have to go over to the Gonzalezes to take a look at old Martin's infected foot. It is some distance down the road and I will not be back in time to vaccinate the pigs. It has to be done this morning because these shots are overdue already, and in the afternoon I have other things planned." Having said that, she hand-combed her short brown hair to the side, grabbed her jacket, her medical supply bag, and went outside where a farmhand held her horse already saddled and ready to go.

"Wait a minute, how much do I have to give them," I called out running after her. "And where is that stuff?"

"One cubic centimeter into the thigh muscle and it is all on the table in the office,"she responded as she mounted her horse.

I stood there for a minute then went to the office. There they were, two rows of little two inch tall glass containers. I had watched my aunt before when she prepared the serum. She poked the needle of the syringe into one bottle sucking the saline solution out and injected it into the other containing the powder with the active agent. A good shake and the injectable serum was ready. That part was easy, but I had never given a shot before. Could I do it? Well, I just had to. I couldn't disappoint Aunt Rita.

Looking through the window I saw three farmhands with their saddled horses sitting around in their ponchos, talking and joking.

"Are you waiting for me to work on the pigs?" I asked them as I stepped out of the house. " Señora Rita told me that we had to vaccinate them this morning."

"Si señorita, we are ready. Do you want us to get your horse?"

"Yes, do that please. You know where my English saddle is. I will be out in a minute."

Back at the office, I collected the little containers, grabbed a spare syringe just in case, placed everything in a brown leather bag I saw hanging on the wall, and went outside.

As we rode, I enjoyed this beautiful day and I think my horse did to judging by his eagerness to move ahead. No prodding was needed. After last week's rain the warm sunshine felt good. Grass glistened still wet with the morning dew. We rode by a field that was being plowed. Blackbirds followed each row having a feast of unearthed worms. The roof of a lean-to steamed as the sun hit the wet wood. The smell of freshly cut grass permeated the air. Cows were in their pasture. It was a peaceful morning, a promising day.

We rode in a single file on the higher and dryer side of the road avoiding big puddles. Soon we arrived at two corrals connected by a narrow passageway. I could see small to medium sized pigs in one of them. Some were digging in the mud, others dozing in the sun huddled together in tight groups on higher ground.

I went to the passage with a gate at both ends and prepared the serum. The farmhands herded the pigs over and the spectacle began. The oink-oinks became louder and louder turning into awful squeals as the pigs ran from side to side, frantic. Pigs are smart and they sensed that something unknown to them was happening. Fear had set in. Two men grabbed the first pig that entered the gangway and used all their strength to hold the struggling animal down so I could do my job. By then the pigs made high pitched ear-piercing noises.

I did not have much time to think before giving the first shot. The men watched me, their expression communicating their worry about my competence: is she going to do it? Does she know how? On the ride here I had remembered a friend saying: "It's like poking into an orange, the outside is hard and then it goes in easy." It was true. It did.

It took just a little over an hour to finish our task. The pigs were now in the connecting corral happily munching on an extra helping of food.

"Well, how did it go?" Aunt Rita asked after returning. "Did you have any problems?"

"Everything went smoothly, the pigs are fine." I answered proudly. "The leftover bottles are in the office. How is old Martin's foot?"

"He'll live."

After a thunderstorm

"Did you know that for our senior trip we will go skiing for a week on the slopes of the Llaima?" one of my classmates asked me, as we walked into the dressing room before gym class.

"No, I did not. When?"

"In a couple of months, and we are going to stay at the large lodge. Are you going?"

"Of course. Would not miss that for anything," I said as we were putting on our black gym shorts. "Is the whole class going?"

"Just about and some teachers also as chaperones. Otherwise they would not let us go since we are a co-ed school."

That was exiting news and it made the rounds fast. All senior classes made a trip to somewhere in Chile, I knew that, and I had heard about the Llaima, an active volcano about 10,000 feet high. It was certainly something to look forward to.

Days and weeks went by quickly. I was so busy with school, and homework that I had barely time to eat and sleep. It was a good thing our apartment was within walking distance to school, thus avoiding long commutes and wasted time.

Fall turned into winter and our departure date to the Llaima drew closer. The topic of conversation among us girls drifted more and more toward the trip. Some girls, not interested in skiing, were more concerned about what clothing to take. They intended to sunbathe and watch the boys.

Others, myself included, wanted to make sure we had what was needed to use our skis: the proper wax for different types of snow and good bindings. The leather straps had to be in good repair and not on the verge of braking. My skies were 20-year-old hand-me-downs from my uncle Curt. They were made out of hickory wood, had metal edges and were much too long for me. I could not even reach the tip with my outstretched hand, but I did not care. I was used to them by now, having skied with them for the past three years. For warmth I had new ski pants made out of thick gabardine. The snow did not cling so much to this smooth material.

We were allowed to take only one piece of luggage or a backpack and our skis. This time we did not have to worry about food. This was a nice lodge with a dining room, bathrooms and warm running water. It was a stark contrast to the cabin we had been to a couple of years before.

Finally the day arrived when we were boarding the train to Temuco, a city about 450 miles south of Santiago. From there a bus took us to the lodge. Skis and baggage followed in a truck. The lodge was an impressive looking building about five or six stories high, nestled against a small slope and surrounded by tall Araucaria trees native to Chile.

It took some time for our group of about forty people to retrieve their belongings from the truck and find their respective rooms. It had been a long day and after dinner at 9:30 we all went to bed.

The next day a teacher gave us general instructions, timetables and informed us that a guide had been hired to take us to the summit of the Llaima.

"Who is interested in going?" our head teacher asked. "It will take a good part of the day and we have to carry our skies. As you know there are no ski lifts here. You have still four days to improve your skiing. So, who is interested?"

It was an easy decision for me. I wanted to go. A few other students also raised their hands. When the day finally arrived, we were a group of eight boys and two girls, plus the guide and the teacher.

"Let's go and have breakfast first. We will miss lunch, so you better eat now," our teacher advised us as he walked toward the dining room. We knew he was right and followed. After a hearty breakfast of hash browns, eggs and bacon, we were ready.

It was a beautiful morning, sunny with just a few clouds in the sky, the air crisp, still below freezing. Icicles hanging from the eves glistened in the sunshine. The air was still and not a sound could be heard. It was so peaceful. The tall araucaria trees, having lost their white snowcaps, and smaller bushes were a stark contrast to the white surroundings.

At 7:30 AM we gathered in front of the lodge, anxious to start. The guide gave final instructions and off we went, following him in a single file. Since we were carrying our skis, we left a few paces between each other to avoid getting tangled up with them. The powdery snow swished with each step. In other places, where it had a thin icy crust, it made crunchy sounds. We walked a slow but steady pace leaving a long trail of disturbed snow behind.

As we reached higher altitudes, we could see more of the land below us. All the wonderful slopes we could ski downhill later on presented themselves to us. That thought kept us all going. The steam spewing from the crater was becoming more visible and clearer to the eye. We were now a little further apart from each other, hard uphill walking taking its toll. Our teacher, being the oldest and not so fit anymore, was at the end of the line. The skis were getting heavier and heavier and our shoulders sore.

It was past midday when we climbed the last few meters to the summit.

What a view, what a sight, just breathtaking. It rejuvenated us instantly. Tiredness and exhaustion disappeared. We could see hundreds of miles. Two more snowcapped volcanoes peeked out of the clouds, the Osorno and the Villarica. We had a 360-degree endless view. It was magnificent!

And then there was the sulfur smell coming out of the depth of the mountain. After all, it was a live volcano that had erupted many times in the past. The crater was mostly filled with snow with the exception of one side, where, out of a black hole, steam rose and curled into the sky.

We rested, ate some snow to quench our thirst, and took pictures. And then came the moment we had waited for, the downhill to the lodge. My skis responded beautifully. We zigzagged for a while, slalom-style, carefully avoiding large rocks. At each curve the snow flew high behind us leaving a ski track like a sidewinder snake in the sand. Every so often we stopped to catch our breath and make this downhill last. We were in no hurry. The scenery was beautiful. Pristine snow, untouched by men, glistened in the sun. Further down, where it was less steep, we let the skis run down the slopes in large sweeping curves. An unbelievable feeling! Soon the lodge came into sight in the far distance. A few more little hills and we were back.

This certainly was by far the highlight of the week and I felt like I had conquered the world.

Mapuche indians at the train station in
Temuco barefoot in winter

Volcano Llaima and the lodge

Rhona

THE GYPSY BARON

"Hurry, go to your assigned spots, take your positions," a hushed voice urged us on. "We are about to start," the same voice continued. The lighting on the stage grew dim. Feet shuffled back and forth, clothing rustled and throats were cleared. Here and there a last minute whisper, a cough, then silence. We didn't even dare to breathe. My heart pumped hard and fast and sounded loud in my ears.

On the other side of the crimson red velvet curtain separating us from the audience, the orchestra was getting ready. Musicians fine-tuned their instruments, positioned chairs and music stands to their liking, and took a last glance at the score to refresh their memories and reassure themselves. Muffled sounds of a few notes and scales played on a variety of instruments reached us behind the curtain.

Suddenly there was applause. In my imagination I could see the conductor, dressed elegantly in tails, white dress shirt and bowtie, as he approached his podium in his black patent leather shoes, bow toward the audience and then turn around to face the orchestra. The applause ebbed down, he raised his hand holding the baton and the overture began.

It was opening night of the *Gypsy Baron* by Johann Strauss.

Three months earlier our music teacher called several of us girls back, as we were leaving the classroom.

"Wait, I have to ask you something. An impresario is staging an operetta in German, the Gypsy Baron to be exact. Would you be interested in being part of the chorus? They need about ten to twelve German-speaking girls."

We looked at each other in disbelief. "You mean we would sing on a stage in front of an audience?"

"That is exactly what I mean. We will practice two, three times a week after class right here in this room. The soprano will come from Germany, a tenor from Buenos Aires, and the others are local people. We have over two months until the opening on September 20, in the opera house right here in Santiago. It will be fun. Do you want to do it? Do you want to participate?"

We looked at each other and without hesitation nodded affirmatively. And with that nod our artistic career began.

We practiced for several weeks with our music teacher at the piano. He was a middle-aged man of small stature, slightly balding with pale blue eyes behind his round glasses. We learned the lyrics, sang the many songs over and over again, and he never became impatient or angry when a mistake was made. He gave us confidence. Many melodies were beautiful and also catchy and, without realizing it, I hummed them quite often during the day.

The time came when we had to rehearse with the other singers. We were introduced to the concert agent Ernesto Hall, the lead singer from Germany Dolores Mannerheim who was to sing the role of the gypsy princess, the handsome tenor from Argentina, Eva Krutein, the music coach, and many more participants. At the beginning we gathered a few times in the school auditorium, and then at the opera house itself. We had to get acquainted with the layout of the theater, the stage, get used to the acoustics, lighting and side wings. We had to know where the back entrance was, since this time we were not the audience but the performers. It was all unfamiliar territory for us, our first venture into the theater world behind the curtains.

Before the dress rehearsal we were given our costumes. One set for a typical gypsy, complete with jewelry and headdress, and one for a simple farm-girl. Depending on the scene, we had to change from one to the other, and it had to be done fast.

Then they showed us how to apply our make-up. Our faces were practically re-done.

"I think I have to work on your eyebrows," a helpful person said to me, grabbing a bar of soap. "I will cover them up with this. It's cheap but effective," he explained. "Gypsies and country folks don't have such light skin as you do. We have to give you a tan," And he applied a darker foundation to my face. "We are almost done," he exclaimed, as he drew new arching eyebrows, added eye shadow, dark lipstick and rouge. In no time he had turned me into somebody else.

"Do you like it? You saw how easy it is. Now you can do it yourself," and off he went to his next object without waiting for my reply, comment or thank you.

The general public became aware of the upcoming performance. Articles were printed in the *Condor*, the weekly German newspaper. Posters, announcing the operetta, were displayed at the opera house. They depicted the German singer with her long blond hair in an exotic gypsy outfit. The sale of tickets began. We were given two complimentary ones for our parents.

The thought of being part of this event was exciting, especially when someone approached me with questions and I had most of the answers. It felt great. I felt important.

And now it was opening day. The house was sold out. I peeked through the spy hole in the curtain and saw the mass of people. It gave me goose bumps to see all the faces in the audience. It was both intimidating and challenging. Mostly everybody was seated, only a few latecomers waited for ushers. This was it, the moment we had worked for.

We were at our positions on the stage and waited.

The overture, a musical summary of the operetta, was coming to its end. Applause again and slowly the curtain rose. The prompter was sitting in her box, smiling, as if to give us courage. Beyond her, the conductor was looking at us, his eyebrows raised demanding attention. The orchestra began to play. He raised his arm, held it there for a few seconds pointing the baton at the lead singer. With a swing of his baton he gave her the exactly timed entrance.

My heart pounded, but a few seconds into the music I calmed down. All I had learned was still there. One scene, one beautiful aria followed another. There were many nuances of feelings in the melodies, from fast and happy to slow and heart-gripping sadness. Melancholic gypsy tunes alternated with military beats and tender love songs. They spoke of gypsy girls, hidden treasures, noble heirs and pig farmers, of soldiers and fortune telling, and, of course, the gypsy baron. They all sounded very much alive.

The first act was over, the second, and then the third. After the last tone faded away, there was silence and then thundering applause, turning into a standing ovation. It was proof that we had captured the audience's imagination. There were several curtain calls, bouquets of flowers were given to the main characters, and then the show was over.

Yes, the show was over, as well as my short-lived singing career. But I was filled with pride and joy for having participated in this operetta. It had been a wonderful and unique experience and will be forever engraved in my memory.

COLORED MARBLES

Students from different schools gathered in a hallway of the Universidad de Chile on Alameda Boulevard in downtown Santiago. It was a two-story structure, antique-looking and ornate. A few years back it had received a fresh coat of paint, yellow with white trim. A statue of Andres Bello, the founder of the university, stood in front of the entrance. It was a city landmark.

As I peeked into one of the unoccupied rooms, I found it to be large and the ceiling high, around ten to twelve feet. It was adorned with wide, intricate crown-moldings. Rows of tables and chairs filled the room. Through the tall windows on one side sunshine flooded in, making it more inviting.

High school was over and done with. Now we were here to be tested for the *bachillerato*, the equivalent of an entrance exam to a college or university.

We could choose between several College majors. I picked humanities, with a minor in biology, which meant that I had to pass tests in Spanish, history and geography of Chile, German or French, chemistry, and biology or botany. German or French and biology or botany were decided by pure luck. We pushed a button and a colored marble came down a chute deciding one's fate, for example a black marble for German and a red one for French.

Some students, still studying, paced up and down the corridor concentrating on the open books they were holding, oblivious of what was going on around them. The sound of their shoes hitting the tiled floor resonated throughout the hallway. Other students appeared nervous, some even close to tears. What if I don't make it, what if I flunk? Those were the questions written on their faces. Anxiety spread; everybody was tense. For many the outcome was very important, more so, if they wanted to continue their studies at a higher level.

After receiving the two assignments decided by the colored marbles, I looked for my friend, Gretel. We had been studying together and quizzing each other on the different subjects. She was a very good student, disciplined, dependable and hard working. I liked her calmness. Nothing could upset her.

"Wouldn't you know I got French," I called out to her when I saw her brown ponytail in the crowd. "It's a fifty-fifty chance and I had to get that. Me, the one from Germany. What bad luck!"

"I got German and I am happy about that, but they will quiz me on botany and that is not my strong subject. It makes me uncomfortable and nervous. It's a good thing that I attended those evening classes with Mrs. Fonck."

"Oh, you will do fine, don't worry," I assured her, giving her a hug.

"Well, I don't know. I hope so. I wish we could get this over with. Waiting and just standing around doesn't help. And don't you think that they could have let us wear regular clothes instead of our uniforms? Everybody knows what school we are from."

"Well, it's not that bad. Anyways, it is the last time," I answered as we were going down the hall to join our other classmates.

School uniforms are mandatory in Chile. All public school students are dressed in navy blue with white blouses and shirts for girls and boys respectively. Private schools can select their own colors and designs, complete with initials or emblems of the different institutions. We girls had two sets of outfits: brown wool jumper with the initials DS (Deutsche Schule, GermanSchool) embroidered on the upper left hand side of it, along with a beige blouse and dark brown sweater, for winter, and a beige short-sleeved cotton dress for summer. The boys wore brown pants, white shirts and brown jackets, also with the initials DS.

In our senior year we were about fifty students divided into two groups: class A and class B. Now we were all together waiting for what was to come. We had been scheduled for nine o'clock, and now it was fifteen minutes past that and nothing was happening. We were getting impatient. But then a few jokesters got together and made fun of the situation. We began to have a good time, laughing and cheering them on. We relaxed and forgot all about the exams. It was the best medicine for our frayed nerves.

Ten minutes later a voice interrupted us by calling out: "Estudiantes del Colegio Aleman a la sala numero cinco." (German school students go to room five).

Fun was over.

Room five was just down the hall. What a coincidence; it was the one I had peeked into earlier. Now the sun was almost gone, making the room look dreary. Getting a closer look I saw the desks to be quite worn and ink-stained. Initials carved into the dark wood here and there were reminders of previous students. The desks had to be quite old since they still had the round holes on the top corner for the old-fashioned inkwells. We didn't need those any more. Now we were using fountain pens, and if the brand was Parker, we really were lucky, more so, if our name was engraved on the body of the pen.

We took our seats.

A gray-haired skinny man was standing at a large desk in the front of the classroom working on a stack of papers. He looked sick and had dark circles around his eyes.

"This testing will be on history and geography of Chile. I will hand out the papers now and you have ninety minutes to finish the test," the man announced. "No talking is allowed," he continued. "You can use pencil or ink it does not matter which. When you are done, put your papers here on the desk and then you can leave."

I didn't think he was the teacher, more a clerk filling in to get us started. He was wearing black sleeve covers over his jacket sleeves. They started at his wrist and ended above the elbow, with elastic at both ends. Clerks wore those to protect their clothing, and maybe their only jacket, from daily wear and tear inflicted by desk surfaces.

Sure enough, shortly after we had the questionnaires, a teacher made his entrance. He had a more authoritative look about him. His trousers had sharp creases; he wore cufflinks matching the clip on his tie, and his black wavy hair, graying at the temples, gave him the look of a distinguished college professor. He deposited his briefcase on the front desk and introduced himself.

"I am Mario Duarte and I will be here for the duration of the test. You were given instructions already. The essay about the war between Chile and Peru represents half of your grade, so do well on that. Any Questions?" Silence.

"Bueno, then you can start," and with that he began walking slowly down the aisles between the desks. Up and down, and up and down. Sometimes I got a whiff of his after shave lotion as he passed by.

After finishing the test, we gathered outside the room. We compared answers. Some had been easy, others hard. In general we all thought that we probably had passed. One down, four to go.

That same day I took two more tests, biology was in writing, and the other, French, was oral. How I dreaded that one when they called my name. I had a good teacher during the last three years, strict, demanding good study habits, but I would have been much happier with German.

When I came out of the classroom after being quizzed, I was approached by several students wanting to know every detail of the examination. "What did they ask? Did you have to translate something? Did they talk to you in French? How about grammar and conjugations?" I answered as many questions as I could and left. It had been a long day and I had to come back the next morning. I needed to go home and review my notes for the remaining two examinations.

The next day I felt much better. Now I knew the place. It was more familiar and my nerves were calmer. I felt sorry for the newcomers who had this first-day experience ahead of them. After taking my remaining tests in Spanish and chemistry, I felt a great relief. It was finally over.

I had to wait a whole week before I could pick up the test results at my school. It was a very long week filled with a variety of emotions, doubts, regrets of not having studied more intensely, then cheerfulness for having done it at all. Finally the day came when I went to pick up my results. Was it a good sign that the teacher was smiling as she handed me the envelope? My heart was pounding. I tore open the brown envelope. . and . . yes, yes I did it. Now I had it in black and white, I had passed. Not on the top, but right in the middle. Good enough for me. To my surprise, my best grade was in Spanish.

I gathered my uniforms and took the bundle to an office at the school where parents with lower incomes could get these at low cost, or even for free.

No more brown uniforms for me.

DECISIONS

A few days after my final exams I took a train to the south of Chile to visit my Aunt Rita and Uncle Harry, just as I had done the last couple of years. It was summertime and I loved it there. The fresh air, the simplicity of farm life, and the open space were to my liking. I loved the uncomplicated ways with no cars, no electricity and no telephone. It did not bother me that we had to use an outhouse hidden behind some bushes or that I was third in line in the weekly bathwater after my aunt and uncle. I loved to touch the soft muzzle of my horse as I fed him an apple, and the smell of freshly cut alfalfa. The air was filled with sounds of happy birds, and insects buzzing around in search of nectar. A terrier mix named Marulli was my daily companion, following me wherever I went.

Even an occasional rain did not diminish my happiness. We lit the large fireplace with small twigs at first, following up with big logs. The wet wood hissed and crackled. That, along with the sound of the raindrops hitting the windows, and the howling wind, made me appreciate the cozy living room. Marulli's off and on yelping, as he slept next to me dreaming of past adventures made it even better.

It was a good life even though I was not just sitting around admiring the beautiful cloud formations; I was also helping my aunt with her chores. Every day we churned a big batch of butter. In the evening a truck picked up the full milk cans from all the farms along the road and also our butter, and drove them to town. We fed the leftover nonfat milk to the calves and I also helped vaccinate the many pigs, calves and cows.

Aunt Rita was a horse lover and kept a constant eye on them to make sure they were in good health, had no sores on their backs from rubbing saddles or, God forbid, swollen ankles after a full day's work. If they were limping, we took them to the close-by lake to stand in the cold water. And of course the horseshoes had to be perfect and their coats clean and well brushed.

Every so often someone arrived on horseback to ask her to attend to a sick person, as she was known in the area for having some medical knowledge and the willingness to help. In those instances we grabbed a small satchel she had for those occasions, filled with a variety of pills, salves, bandages, and scissors, and headed out to the place requiring assistance. To reach a real doctor one had to travel a whole day to the next city, so everyone was happy to have her, especially because she didn't charge a dime for her advice and any medication.

On weekends we sometimes got together with neighbors, played cards, or just talked about the current events while sipping a glass of wine. If someone in the area slaughtered an animal, we sometimes had a barbeque, but not often. The larger animals like cows, pigs, goats and sheep were mostly raised for sale. Our protein in those days came from chicken, fish from the nearby lake, and milk products.

But, as much as I liked it there, it was not forever. I knew that. I had to do some thinking about what my future would be. Mom and Dad had never talked to me about that. They had not suggested either school or work, or made it clear what they wanted or expected from me. I was given very little guidance, if any. When I mentioned that I wanted to visit Aunt Rita after the testing was done, they thought it was a great idea and that was it.

Maybe I should not have come here. Maybe it was a mistake. What was I thinking! Now the registration period for the university was over for the year, so for the immediate future it had to be a job.

"What are you daydreaming about?" my aunt called out as she approached me.

"Oh, nothing special," I answered, rising from the step of the front porch where I had been sitting.

"Ok, then, guess what? Next weekend we will go over to the Fuenzalida's house. It is a good stretch up the road. You haven't met them yet," my aunt announced as she got off her horse. "I just saw Maria and she invited us. She will send somebody to pick us up in their jeep so we don't have to ride."

"What is the occasion? Is it somebody's birthday?" I inquired.

"No, they expect company from Santiago. We can use some news from the outside world. Our last newspaper is almost a week old." And with that Aunt Rita went into the house, having taken off her dusty riding boots at the front door.

I liked the idea. It was something to look forward to.

The days went by quickly since it was harvest time. We were out in the fields to watch the progress of alfalfa and oats being cut. Uncle Harry was happy. No rain was on the horizon, and in a few days the hay could be gathered and stored in the barn. Now it was the time to reap the fruit of all the hard work done in early spring.

"They are picking us up at noon, be ready," Aunt Rita reminded me in the morning.

"Should I wear a dress or just my jeans?" I asked.

"You can wear whatever you want. It's a casual affair."

I remembered then, that I didn't even bring a dress, just a red skirt I had sewn before coming here. That would work with a white blouse and my white sandals.

When we arrived at the large farm house, the guests had all gathered underneath an extensive pergola covered with grapevines. It was shady, the light breeze comfortable. Most of the neighbors were there and a few people I didn't know. There was lots of food and drinks for every taste and the conversation was lively. Aunt Rita introduced me to Maria, the lady of the house, and her husband. I thanked them for the invitation and the fact that we were picked up. Otherwise it would have been a very long ride. Then we mingled with the guests and had a good time.

"Buenas tardes, señorita," a man's voice said to me from behind.

"Buenas tardes," I answered as I turned around to see who he was. I was looking at a nicely dressed man in city garb. He was clean shaven, probably in his mid fifties. He had a distinguished look and seemed to be very sure of himself. He must be the visitor from Santiago I thought to myself.

"My name is Mario Alessandri. I am a friend of the Fuenzalidas, and I am here for a very short vacation. I was told that you are señora Rita's niece."

"Yes, you are right. My name is Rhona and I am also here on vacation, but mine is a little longer. I have a reservation on the nocturno (the nightly sleeper train) for March first so I can stay three more weeks."

"You are lucky!"

"Maybe lucky in that respect, but I have problems too. I just finished high school, passed the bachillerato (university entrance examination) and now I have to look for a job. That might not be so easy."

'You are smart. I don't think you will have any difficulty finding one."

We talked for a little while longer, and then joined the others.

When Aunt Rita and I were ready to go home, Mario approached me again. "When you're back in Santiago, come and see me. For now enjoy your stay here." With that he gave me a business card and left.

On the card it said: Banco de Credito e Inversiones, Mario Alessandri, Vice President.

I knew then that I had a job.

And I did.

"This is impossible! You can't draw from the business account more than you put in. I have told you that repeatedly." Dad was upset with his partner, and with reason. "Wait until more money comes in before you write checks, and besides we need more important things than the ones you are buying."

Dad and Mr. Dunker had established a partnership where dad was doing most of the actual work and Mr. Dunker, fluent in Spanish, was more the representative and business getter. They had rented a two-room office on the second floor of a building close to downtown Santiago. Parking was no problem since the building was facing a big square. On the opposite side of it was the Chilean Opera House. During the Opera season I was a frequent spectator there and loved the beautiful music.

Building up the business from nothing had been a challenge. They were repairing or building anything electrical, small or large, and needed many tools and instruments.

In time the business became profitable and they had plenty of work. One day they were offered the representation of electronic organs from "Hammond" in Chicago. Not that there was a big market for expensive organs in a country as small as Chile, but maybe two or three sales were possible.

"We received a call from the office of the President of Chile, Gonzalo Videla!" Carlos Dunker exclaimed happily one day as Dad entered the office. "He is interested in an organ for the cathedral in La Serena, his hometown."

"Well, well, that is good news. I guess our advertising worked," Dad exclaimed. "We will have to set up a work schedule for this project and get in touch with Chicago. I want this to go smoothly."

At a subsequent meeting with President Videla himself, it was decided to fly with him to La Serena in the presidential airplane nicknamed "El Canela". The actual location within the Cathedral, where the organ was to be placed, had to be inspected and exact measurements were needed.

All difficulties were worked out and the organ was installed. Representatives from the Hammond Company came to Chile to participate in the inauguration. It was a big event for the small city of La Serena.

In 2006 I was in Chile with a group of people visiting the northern part of that country. Our itinerary also took us to La Serena, now a much bigger city after 50 years. I found the cathedral. Unfortunately it was closed, but, talking to people, I learned that the organ is still in use today. I actually heard the chimes indicating four o'clock in the afternoon. I was very proud of that fact and Dad would have been happy to know that he had done good work.

Word spread and Cardinal Silva from Santiago heard about this organ and wanted one for Talca, a city south of Santiago. This second sale gave the partnership a good boost.

All went well, but spending problems with Carlos Dunker continued and Dad was entertaining the idea of ending the partnership. Besides, he could not see himself working like this for the rest of his life. He needed to establish something that would support him and Mom in their old age. Chile did not have a "social security system." Pension plans did not exist. What would happen if he got sick and was unable to work?!

In 1955 coincidentally one of their customers offered Dad a piece of property in Malloco, a small village about 20 miles from downtown Santiago. The piece of land was more like a big lot, but the 2500 square meters were just enough to set up a small egg ranch with 4500 hens, which at that time were producing a good income.

We had several family discussions pondering this opportunity. Was that it? Should we do that? What do we know of poultry and hens in particular? Nothing, but we can learn. They lay eggs and more eggs! We sell the eggs! One man can feed the hens and do the work. How can that be so difficult? Let's do it! And so we did.

The seller of the property, Mr. Wegertseder, a fellow from the Bavarian region of Germany who had immigrated in the early 1930s, offered us all kinds of help since he had a similar "egg" business just down the street.

The piece of property had a rectangular shape and was enclosed by a block wall. One half of a duplex stood next to the property line on one side. It had been built for a worker to live in and consisted only of two rooms, a minute kitchen, a toilet and a small porch. There was no bathtub or shower. The floors were cement and the walls barely white washed. At the far end of the lot on the same side were two storage rooms, and the rest of the grounds were weeds.

Where do we start???

It was somewhat overwhelming, so much needed to be done.

Paint and new wood floors made a big difference. We were ready to move. We had a roof over our heads. Luckily it was summer, since a garden hose hanging from an overhead hook served as our shower.

Dad continued working in Santiago. I kept my job at a bank where I had started just a few months ago right after finishing school. I worked less hours than Mom at the photo-shop and so we decided that she should quit and stay home to keep a watchful eye on the place.

Workers were busy enlarging the bathroom as well as adding a good-sized kitchen. The old kitchen became a coat closet. The two rooms in the back of the lot were prepared to receive the first batch of chicks. More open enclosures were added along the back wall for when those chicks grew.

"Look what I brought you," Dad said one Saturday afternoon when he was coming back from Santiago. "Come outside and see what it is." Mom and I rushed outside and there was the cutest German Shepard puppy. We named her Bella and she became our well-respected guardian of the property.

In time Dad dissolved the partnership and dedicated himself to the work at home. Several rows of structures were built where the cages for the hens were hanging. We had only one hen in each cage. A storage room for eggs was added, and Dad built an egg-sorting machine, relieving me from my daily evening job of weighing each egg separately. Now they were carried on a narrow conveyer belt over three separate calibrated scales and fell into the compartment corresponding to their weight. This machine was so efficient that Dad built several more and sold them.

When the number of chickens increased as well as the feed consumption we acquired a truck. Buying all the ingredients for the chickenfeed separately and mixing them in a large mixing machine saved quite a bit of money. A well was dug and the water pumped into a large basin on top of a high structure. Gravity brought the water to the different faucets.

Dad did most of the work himself since he knew everything about motors and electronics, some plumbing, and was good at problem solving. Mom was like the mother hen. She vaccinated the baby chicks, tended to the sick hens, gave shots and watched for signs of disease. A worker did the feeding, cleaning and in time learned the basic operation. I think Mom and Dad were happy during that time. They did not fear challenges and were always striving for good results with perseverance and hard work.

The operation became quite automated, as they had wanted it to be.

After a few years, the house was remodeled, adding a second story with a balcony and another room downstairs. Mom had planted a few fruit trees, put in a lawn, and started her roses. The patio was covered by an arbor where grapevines grew, providing shade and fruit in summertime.

Dad even had or made time for his hobby: ham operator. He talked to half the world at different times of the day or night. His knowledge of electronics allowed him to give operational advice to others, and soon he was known as "abuelito Uli" (grandpa Uli) all over South America. He also participated in a voluntary emergency service formed by a chain of ham operators along the length of Chile. Every day they called in, kept in touch and were ready to act when needed.

The beginning of this "adventure" in Malloco was rough, with a lot of ups and downs, but in the end the result was good and showed that with perseverance, determination and hard work everything is possible.

Kitchen under construction

Future henhouse with cages and the finished product

130

Mom at work and Bella watching

President Videla with white hat

Dad in the middle

SCOOTERS AND CARS

I was living in Santiago, Chile, in the late fifties and for two years had been the proud owner of a Lambretta. It was a time when scooters were "in", because they were affordable and available. Shipments from Italy came frequently, and there was hardly any waiting time to drive one off the lot.

Car imports did exist, but a very high luxury tax was imposed on them, doubling the sticker price of a car. They were only for the very rich.

People were happy to have scooters. They took them to where they wanted to go, use of gasoline was minimal, and the parking was no problem. Two wheels were better than none.

One evening, after coming home from work, my dad showed me the *Condor*, a German weekly newspaper, pointing to an add.

" I saw this in today's paper. A man is selling his old car, a Fiat 500 Topolino. For some reason it's partially disassembled and because of that, he is selling it for less. I can take a look. Maybe I can put it together. I think it would be a good idea for you to move up to a car, and sell the scooter."

"That would certainly make life a lot easier," I answered enthusiastically. "Remember it has to be cheap. But do you think you can do it, Dad, with all the other projects you're working on?"

"I make time. Don't worry about that."

I knew he would say that. He loved to work with engines, and everything else related to cars, or anything mechanical for that matter. He had an inventive mind and could find acceptable solutions to just about everything.

As it turned out, we were able to pick up the car in a few days, but it was another couple of months before Dad had made it drivable.

What a transformation it had gone through. The engine was overhauled, the brakes replaced, and a few hoses changed. With its new coat of light blue paint it looked like new. The rims were a little beat up and a hubcap was missing but I did't care. The handbrake had only a handle for show, the rest was missing. I overcame this problem by just parking the car in first gear to prevent it from rolling away. The important thing was that now I had four wheels under me and a roof over my head. Bad weather and rain did not bother me anymore.

Dad showed me how to drive with a manual transmission and gave me some pointers. I found it easy to transition from scooter to car and Dad quickly felt comfortable riding with me.

I obtained my drivers license with no problems. It was only a matter of going to an office to apply for it and pay the dues. No written or driving tests were required.

I sold my Lambretta and began to enjoy my little Topolino. It took me everywhere I wanted to go comfortably. My hair was not flying in the wind, I could dress any way I wanted, I was warm, and I had room to stash bags inside the car when I bought something. It obviously did not compare to bigger and newer vehicles, but I was delighted with what I had.

I learned the basics about car maintenance, how to check the oil and water on a weekly basis, and how to use the jack to change a tire. The training came in handy. Tires were not readily available in Chile and I had to make use of my knowledge several times until I found and bought a couple of new tires.

In those days parking spaces were not marked along the streets. One car just parked behind the other, often leaving very little space in between. One day I had parked in front of my workplace. When I left the office in the evening, I discovered my Topolino squeezed in between two big cars with no room to get out. It was trapped.

"It looks like you're in a bind," a couple of co-workers said, a big grin on their faces. "You can't wait here until the other cars leave. That could take hours. Let's see what we can do." Having said that they went to the underground garage of the building and came back with two maintenance guys. They all rolled up their sleeves, positioned themselves two in front and two in back and proceeded to lift my car out. Just like that!

A group of spectators had crowded around watching the activities. We all had a good laugh after the task was accomplished. Having a small and light car had its advantages.

Next time I thought it would be better to park in the underground garage even though I had a vague suspicion that it was for the higher-ups of the Bank, where I worked, and their Cadillacs.

Sure enough.

"Señorita, you can't park here. All the spaces are taken. There is no room."

"Not even a little? It is small car," I pleaded.

"*No, lo sentimos mucho*, señorita. You can't stay here."

Disappointed I turned around toward the exit and immediately had a bad feeling. This was not good, not good at all. The driveway out of the garage was short but very steep and there was no room to pick up speed in advance. I felt like David confronting Goliath. I tried it in second gear, then changed it to first and managed about three quarters of the way. Then I had to disengage and roll back. Turning around in my seat I saw the two garage attendants looking at me in disbelief. *What is she doing* was written all over their faces

"Let me try again in reverse. It is a stronger gear," I called over to them.

I turned around and began backing up the incline. I almost made it …. but not quite. How embarrassing! I felt my heart beating faster. What was I going to do?!

"Drive up in first señorita, and we will push. You will make it then," they assured me. And I did, never to try an underground garage again.

Even with my car's limitations I was very happy to own it. I was a careful driver and never had an accident. The little car took me to my workplace, drove me to the beach, and shuttled me to my friends' houses. Best of all, it let me enjoy my new-found mobility.

I had the Topolino for about two years before selling it to come to the United States. My sadness about seeing it go was overshadowed by my anticipation of my upcoming trip.

The little Fiat will always have a special place in my heart.

GREAT SHAKE

"What's going on?" I cried out as something startled me. By just looking at the hanging lamp in the middle of the room swinging from side to side I knew it was an earthquake. Then I felt it, too. My bed acted like a ship on the high seas, with a few up and down jolts. The tremblers did not want to end. Looking out the window I saw my car, a little two-seater Fiat Topolino, bouncing back and forth. Luckily I had the gears in park otherwise it would have just taken off down our long driveway.

Mom, Dad and I and some neighbors congregated on the street in front of the house. All were visibly shaken and nervous, waiting for an aftershock to come. Just the day before, on May 21, 1960, a national holiday, the city of Concepcion, 270 miles south of Santiago, had experienced an earthquake with a magnitude 8.0. We had felt it in Malloco but it was not nearly as strong as this one.

"That must have been another big quake," one of the women exclaimed. "Are there any damages?"

The general consensus was that nothing had happened besides a few broken dishes, which had slid out of the cupboards and fallen on the floor.

"I wonder where the epicenter was?" somebody else was asking. "It cannot be very far from here, because it shook so hard."

"We have to wait for the news. I am sure there will be a special report any time now," Dad said as he went to inspect our property more in depth. He did not want any unpleasant surprises with broken pipes and leaks.

We talked some more and listened to all the comments. Everybody had something to tell from previous earthquakes, but since apparently there was no aftershock coming, we went inside.

Later in the afternoon the first news was transmitted over the radio. We all stayed close by to hear the latest. We did not want to miss any of it. The epicenter was 100 miles off the coast of Chile between Valdivia and Puerto Montt, about 700 miles south of Santiago. It was of a magnitude 9.5. It was the largest seismic event in the world recorded instrumentally. Loss of life was in the thousands. It generated one of the most destructive Pacific-wide tsunamis with waves as high as 25 meters. They reached the Chilean coast within 10-15 minutes and took 15 hours to travel to the Hawaiian Islands, a distance of 6,000 miles. Japan also was affected, as well as New Zealand.

"Dad come here, they'll have another report." I called out. "Hurry! Mom you to, we can't miss any of this."

"We are coming, we are coming," they responded.

We gathered around the radio, which dad had built himself. He used several speakers and it sounded wonderful. But at this moment I did not care about the sound, we just wanted to hear the latest information.

The news was getting worse and worse. One-third of the city of Valdivia sank into the Pacific. Rock falls and landslides occurred in the Andes. The river San Pedro, which was the outlet of Lake Riñihue, was blocked. The water rose, inundating several villages. A channel had to be built quickly to reconnect the river with the lake, circumventing this dam formed by an avalanche of dirt. They worked feverishly day and night but there was the big question: What would happen when they severed the link between the channel and the lake? Would the force of the unleashed water cause more destruction downstream then anticipated? Would the sudden torrential flow of water crush everything in its way? Nobody knew the answer; it just had to be done.

Two days later, on May 24th the volcano Puyehue erupted, spewing rocks and ashes. It was like hell on earth!

A few more days went by and the digging continued. Then came the critical moment of opening the faucet, so to speak. All Chile was glued to the radio. Would it work? It just had to after this immense effort of digging around the clock. Another half hour and we would know. And then came the good news: the river was flowing at high speed but not causing any problems.

All Chile cheered! Neighbors had congregated out front again.

"Did you hear the latest? Is it not wonderful that all turned out well? I just knew they could do it and they did!" The excitement made us all talk at once.

In the meantime the American Red Cross had arrived with aid in the form of blankets, food, tents, medical supplies, doctors and engineers. All their efforts were written about and applauded in the newspapers on a daily basis. People were tremendously grateful for their help, and more so, since that help came quickly and spontaneously.

Every evening we listened to the news and were amazed at the devastation this quake and the following tsunami had caused. Aftershocks continued for weeks.

These happenings brought back memories of the formation of a new volcano close to Lake Ranco, maybe 50 miles south of Lake Riñihue. It happened a few years before. My Aunt Rita lived not far from the eruption site and we were wondering if she was all right. There were no phones in that area. We did not know the exact details until weeks later when she came for a visit.

"You should have seen us crawling on the street," she said laughing. "The ground shook so bad, that we could not drive the truck and had to get out of the cabin. We looked like babies learning to walk." Aunt Rita could find humor in everything.

"What about the new volcano?" I asked.

Aunt Rita became very serious. One could tell that this was the bad part of her experience.

"It was a small volcano but with a lot of spewing power. It rained ashes for days. All the ranches in the valley were covered by a layer of about two feet of that stuff, killing everything underneath. Bigger animals were filling their lungs with these toxins. Soon we saw dead cattle everywhere, their bloated bellies getting bigger and bigger. The whole area had suffocated. Not a pretty sight! And no rain to wash it away."

We were shocked by her story and so glad that she had escaped injury!

Living in Chile one has to accept the fact that this country has hundreds of dormant and not so dormant volcanoes, and eruptions will occur. Earthquakes are also to be expected since Chile is located over the meeting point of the Chile Ridge oceanic plate and South American Plate.

Date	Location	Richter Magnitude	Seismic Moment Magnitude
May 22, 1960	Chile	8.5	9.5
Mar 28, 1964	Alaska	8.4	9.2
Mar 9, 1957	Aleutians	8.1	9.1
Nov 4, 1952	Kamchatka	8.2	9.0
Dec. 26, 2004	Sumatra	N/A	9.0
Jan 31, 1906	Ecuador	8.2	8.8
Feb 4, 1965	Aleutians	8.2	8.7
Nov 11, 1922	Chile	8.3	8.5
Mar 2, 1933	Japan	8.5	8.4
Aug 15, 1950	India-China	8.6	
Dec 16, 1920	N. China	8.6	

Source: K. Abe, Magnitudes and Moments of Earthquakes, in *Global Earth Physics, A Handbook of Physical Constants*, American Geophysical Union Reference Shelf Volume 1, p. 206-213. Seismic moment magnitudes determined by recalculation from seismic records for events prior to 2004.

The December 2004 Sumatra event is the first Magnitude 9.0 event since the general adoption of the seismic moment magnitude scale; the old Richter Scale is no longer applied to such events.

TRAVEL PLANS

It was a beautiful spring morning in September of 1960. It was sunny and the birds were chirping. The strong fragrance of orange blossoms came in through the open window. The citrus trees were loaded with flowers promising a good crop.

My parents and I were sitting in our nook having a leisurely breakfast, and making plans for the day. Dad was on his second cup of coffee. The aroma still hung in the air. Mom was giving tidbits of buttered toast to Bella, our German shepherd. She always sat on the floor on the same spot halfway leaning against the wall. The wallpaper had already darkened there from dirt and dust in her fur. She waited. She was patient. She knew that eventually she would get some bread. Our cat was also part of the group. The only difference was that he acted very demanding and not shy at all. Meowing loudly, he badgered our nerves. He jumped on our laps, reminding us of his presence, and actually tried to snatch pieces of cheese from our plates. Finally, we gave in. He got his treat and was put outside. We loved him when he slept, curled up on a chair on his favorite pillow, a new one of course, one we had just bought.

Dad finished his coffee as he was glancing at his treasured quartz wristwatch lying on the table, permanently. "This is a good watch," he said, "and all the things it can do!" It had three knobs on one side and one on the other for different functions. It was a novelty in those days, and one of the first ones on the market. He had never worn it. He just admired it and showed it off to visitors. Every so often, he compared the time to the official Greenwich-time, and always was surprised and amazed at its accuracy.

As my mother was about to clear the table I beckoned her to sit down for a moment and wait. "I want to take a trip somewhere," I said. "I would like to go to America. Maybe I can visit Vita in Rockford, Illinois. We have kept in touch over the years and she has invited me several times." Vita was a friend from Hohenfeld, Germany, who had married an American soldier and subsequently followed him to America.

Mom and Dad looked at me and then at each other, smiling, like they had expected something like that for some time.

"So you want to see the world."

"Well, we have talked so much about America lately. I know a lady who just came back from there and she loved it," I answered. "I have money saved up. I can manage."

"Let's talk about it tonight. Do you have any idea how long you want to travel? And what about your job?" Dad asked as he was going toward the door to let the dog out.

"I don't know how long I will be gone. I'll visit Vita and play it by ear. And regarding my job, I will quit. I can get another one when I get back. That's no problem."

"Sounds interesting. Let's talk tonight. I have to fix the brakes of the truck now. Tomorrow I need to pick up a load of fish meal," and with that he went outside to work on his truck.

America was always thought of as the country of prosperity, of plenty, where everything was available. Jobs, good pay, and the necessities of life were immediately obtainable. People could buy used cars for very little. In Chile automobiles were considered a luxury item and import duties were extremely high. They actually doubled the cost of a car. Therefore pre-owned cars kept their value much longer than in the U.S.A. Washing machines and dryers were affordable in America and almost nonexistent in Chile. Washing was done by hand. Clothing too was much cheaper. In Chile readymade clothing was limited. One had a favorite seamstress who sewed the dresses, blouses and skirts, even coats. And besides, the almighty dollar was king. People in Chile collected dollar bills instead of having a savings account in pesos. Inflation was high and the peso had been devaluated several times.

"So, now what about the trip," my dad asked in the evening, as we sat at the table, eating a light meal. "Do you have any specific plans?"

"I thought of taking a ship to Panama, cross over to Miami by plane, and then continue on by bus. This is the most economical way to go. There is an Italian ship leaving Valparaiso the middle of December."

"Sounds pretty good to me, what do you think?" he asked, turning to my mom.

"I think it's a great idea," she answered. "You could call Irmgard Tidow, when you get to Lima. We have not heard from her in years. You remember her, she was with us on the *Reina del Pacifico*." And already thinking ahead and making plans, she continued, "We will have a going-away party and invite our friends for a BBQ."

And so it was decided.

The party was a great success. Family and friends came, a few people from my work and some classmates of mine from school. A pig roasted over a big fire. Picnic tables and benches were set up underneath the grape arbor and we emptied the egg-storage-room for dancing. Dad had set up the music and picked the records. He had a good ear for dance music and rhythm, but I had never seen him on the dance-floor. Everybody had fun, ate and drank, and stayed way past midnight.

A few days later my parents and I left for the port of Valparaiso. I had booked passage on the steamship Americo Vespucci to depart on December 7, 1960. The time had come to embark.

"Good bye, I love you. Bye, bye," I called out at two figures standing on the pier, as I leaned against the railing of an Italian ship. I waved my parents goodbye for as long as I could see them. Soon they seemed like two little specks in the distance and then disappeared completely. I took a deep breath and turned around. Now I was on my own. It was exciting and at the same time somewhat intimidating. This was not a trip to see my aunt in the south of Chile, where all was familiar. No, I was going to a diffcrent country all-together and not with an organized tour. I was going by myself. But I just knew that all would work out, and I was ready to reach for new horizons.

It felt like ages ago that I decided to take a trip, and, now here I was. This ship was smaller in size, took on some cargo, and had fewer passengers than the *Reina del Pacifico*. It sailed along the coast up to Panama, where I had booked a flight to Miami, Florida.

The small cabin had bunk beds against two opposite walls and some space for luggage. Bathrooms were down the hallway. I had not met my roommates yet, and curiosity made me return to the cabin. There was Jane, an American lady, with her two teenage daughters settling in on the three remaining beds. They were on their way home to California. They had been missionaries in Chile for the Church of God for the past two years.

Luckily we got along well, since we had to live together for the next ten days or so. We passed the time playing games, reading and going on shore when the captain allowed it. In Callao, the port of Lima, Peru, I called our friend Irmgard. Her husband answered the phone. He hesitated a long time before speaking again. To me, this silence was like a warning of bad things to come. I was very uneasy. He then proceeded to tell me that two years ago Irmgard had been in a car accident and had died instantly. I was stunned. So that was the reason we didn't hear from her, I thought to myself. I felt bad for him and also for having to tell Mom. She had liked her cheerfulness and friendly nature.

As we sailed along, it was becoming clear to Jane and me that we would miss our planes. The ship was already two days behind schedule, and we had traveled only half the distance. There was no way it could make up the lost time during the remainder of our trip. Jane was not worried. She had friends stationed on a military base in the Canal Zone of Panama, and was sure that we all could stay with them, me included. And that's exactly what happened.

It was a community of white two-story houses. The red roofs had very wide overhangs to provide shade and keep the interior as cool as possible. The first floors had the same size overhang protruding from the walls above the windows and continuing all around the houses. They looked like big awnings. Exotic-looking plants decorated the grounds. Many were in full bloom and we were engulfed by their strong fragrance. Two or three blocks away, the dense tropical jungle started. It was midday when we arrived. The hot and humid air was still; not a breeze could be felt. It dulled the senses.

Jane's friends also belonged to the Church of God. Late that afternoon they asked me if I wanted to come along to one of their services not too far away. I accepted. I wanted to see as much as I could. It turned out to be an interesting experience. The atmosphere in the big hall was happy and very relaxed. People from all walks of life were present, singing lively tunes accompanied by tambourines and an accordion. It was more like a social gathering interrupted briefly by a sermon, some short speeches and many amens and hallelujahs. It was totally different from what I had seen in Catholic or Lutheran churches.

The next morning trash was to be picked up by the city. All the containers were at the curb. From Chile I was used to seeing hoards of stray dogs search the containers for scraps of food and making a mess doing so. Well, here in Panama, monkeys replaced the dogs. They jumped from one trashcan to the other, making screeching noises, chasing each other for the best morsels, and then quickly disappearing into the jungle. They were considered a nuisance one had to live with.

That day I had my first American-style breakfast: a choice of cereal or pancakes. I tried both because cereal was unknown to me and the pancakes were different also. The ones I had growing up were similar to crepes and eaten only as dessert.

Well-fed and energetic, we all drove to the airport, when it started to rain. It rained so hard that traffic came to an abrupt standstill. After three or four minutes, everybody continued on as if nothing had happened. These downpours come several times a day during the rainy season, contributing to the high humidity.

I was lucky to get a window seat on a flight to Miami leaving in a couple of hours. Jane and her daughters had to wait another day for their connecting flight to California. I thanked those good-hearted people for all their kindness and hospitality. Not everybody would have taken in a total stranger!

All four propellers started with no problem and I was on my way. This was my first trip on an airplane that I could remember. My very first flight was in Estonia.

I was just 10 days old. Dad picked my mom and me up from the hospital in his single-engine plane he had built himself. It was just a short flight, but I made the news in Estonia as being their youngest passenger on an airplane.

Now, on my way to Miami, I watched the wings of the plane right below my window. They were not rigid at all. With every little turbulence they came to life and moved up and down. I just hoped that all those rivets along the wings would hold!

Next to me sat a Peruvian girl in her early twenties. She had visited her family and now was returning to the U.S.A.

"Do you have a place to stay when we get to Miami?" she asked after a while, as she was eating her sandwich.

"No, I don't. But I am sure that there is a hotel somewhere."

"How about sharing a room to keep our cost down? I know a cheap, but clean hotel close to the bus terminals. I stayed there once before."

"Great, let's do that. Since we both continue on with Greyhound, it will be convenient to be so close to the depot."

I was relieved to have somebody to talk to in Spanish on my first day in a strange country. I had many questions and could get some good pointers.

It was not a very long flight and time went by fast. Shortly before landing, a stewardess said something about "American regulations". We could not hear her well. But then we saw her, armed with a couple of aerosol cans, walking along the aisle spraying all the passengers! What was that for? I wondered, as I got my shower. We are not contagious and don't have any flees or lice! I heard many complaints and angry remarks. I, too, was unhappy and annoyed about this treatment. It put a damper on this flight!

We got off the plane and went through customs and the documentation check. All was in order. Now, off to the hotel. We were both tired and longed for a hot shower. That night, my first in America, I slept soundly, interrupted only by some crazy dreams of flying monkeys, popping sounds of rivets joining in with tambourines and accordion, and of stewardesses trying to catch me.

I stayed in Miami for a couple of days to do some sightseeing. I was so shocked to see evidence of segregation between blacks and whites. I saw signs at entrances to restaurants and bathrooms indicating that they were for whites only. So where do blacks go!? How is this possible!? Are we not all human beings? This was all new to me and I could not believe my eyes.

From Miami I took a bus to New York. What a big city! I had never seen such tall skyscrapers. I was impressed by the Empire State Building and the Statue of Liberty. The Rockefeller Center with its ice skating ring reminded me of my ice skating days in Germany, although not amid such nice surroundings. I was astonished seeing the richly decorated Christmas tree with thousands of sparkling lights. New Year's Eve 1960 I was at Times Square watching the crystal ball descend and welcome the New Year. The mass of people was scary. Policemen on horseback tried to keep order. It was impossible to move one way or the other. One just had to follow the crowd. Somebody behind me took the opportunity to pinch my behind. I turned around and slapped his face. I was not accustomed to such treatment. He didn't object or complain, so I assumed it was he who did it. These big crowds were not for me, no matter what the occasion.

A few days later I boarded a Greyhound bus to Rockford, Illinois to see Vita, a friend from Germany I had not seen since 1949. It was January and bitter cold. Close to Akron, Ohio, the bus developed engine problems and we had to wait for a replacement vehicle, which took several hours. As we sat in our seats, it began to snow heavily, and soon a white blanket covered the ground. It had a calming effect on the passengers.

Finally we were transferred to a new bus and after a few hours we arrived safely in Rockford, Illinois. Vita, her husband, John, and their 7-year-old daughter, Monica, picked me up from the bus terminal. Vita had married an Americana soldier in Germany and followed him to this country after his discharge from the army. He was a six-footer, of slender build, and Vita reached only up to his shoulder.

They lived in a small two-story brick house with a huge backyard. Vita was a stay-at-home mom, and we had plenty of time to talk and rehash old times while her husband was on his job as a bricklayer.

"Would you like to go ice fishing?" Vita's husband asked me one day. "The lakes have a thick layer of ice by now and we can try our luck with catching some fish."

"I'd love to. I've never done anything like that before," I replied.

"Good, and we will bring the skates also," Vita interjected. "It can get cold and it will do us good to exercise to warm up."

The next day we drove into Wisconsin to a large lake surrounded by trees. We were not the only ones wanting to try their luck with the fish. Ten-to-fifteen cars were parked on the ice. I even saw a small airplane!

After the hole was made in the ice, we sat around it and waited for the fish to bite. No such luck. A few times we had a nibble but that was all. After an hour or so, Vita, Monica and I decided to do some ice-skating and left John watching the lines. When we came back, we saw that he had caught a fish.

My stay with Vita was very nice and also informative. I got acquainted with the daily life in America. I could tell that hard work and being thrifty paid off more here in America than in Chile. It was a good country to live in.

A few more days and my vacation would come to an end. I had to return to Chile. It had been a memorable time filled with new experiences. I had seen things I had never thought could be possible, like the signs 'For Whites Only,' and that Afro-American people had to sit in the back of the bus.

It had shown me again that travels are very educational, and also that, unfortunately, not everything was perfect in the United States.

SEPTEMBER 1961

It was a hot day in September of 1961. Luckily I had a seat on the shady side of a Continental Trailway bus, which had left Mexico City early in the morning with a final destination of Long Beach, California. There was not one empty seat left. All were taken by an array of people, young and old. They came with picnic baskets and shopping bags that barely fit into the overhead compartments. The initial confusion at boarding, and the subsequent excitement of finally leaving, had subsided. Nerves calmed down.

Impressions of the city, *la capital de Mexico,* had been shared among the travelers, and the homemade food brought along was eaten by now. The smell of garlic drifted through the bus. A bottle of tequila had been passed around in the back. And then it became quiet. Only the monotonous humming of the engine could be heard. Siesta time had taken over. As I was sitting in my window seat, I too fell asleep.

A sudden silence woke us all up. The bus had come to a standstill in a small town.

"Bajense todos (Everybody get off). We will be here for one hour and then continue on," the driver said as he opened the doors.

I grabbed my bag, my jacket, got off the bus, and walked toward some shops on a plaza dominated by a large adobe church. The cobblestone street looked old and worn. The air was hot and dry and the burning sun relentless. A few thirsty bushes and trees along the road were covered with dust. Sleeping dogs took advantage of what little shade they gave. A few horses were tied to a post, their heads hanging low, their tails moving slow to swish away the never-ending flies.

"Buenas tardes, señorita," an old man said, as I stepped into a tiny, dimly lit grocery store. He watched me curiously as I selected a big bag of oranges, some bananas, interesting looking Mexican sweet breads, and a bottle of juice. This should last me for a while, I thought.

"Cuanto es todo esto? (How much is all this?)" I asked, as I pulled out my wallet to pay him.

"Tres pesos cincuenta" the toothless man answered. His chin almost touched his nose.

I counted the money into his dark leathery hand. "Muchas gracias y hasta luego" I said, taking the bag and heading toward the bus.

It was still early. Newcomers replaced passengers, which had arrived at their destinations. The open doors of the cargo compartments of the bus allowed me to see my suitcases. They were still there, and I felt relieved. My seat next to the window was waiting for me. Passengers got on the bus, the driver had a new assistant, and it was still hot, even though all the windows were open.

I had chosen the route through central Mexico. It was shorter than the route along the coast, faster and with less stops, so I was told. Besides I wanted to see the countryside. Closer to Mexico City it had been green, but now it was mostly desert. Now and then decaying adobe shacks and broken down fences could be seen. People had come and gone, leaving all behind. Mother Nature took care of the final destruction, aided by human scavengers.

The two-lane road was going north in an almost straight line, losing itself in the horizon. Every so often there were deep dips in the road. They were almost deep enough to allow cars to become invisible when they were in the middle of a dip.

"What are these dips for, do you know?" I asked the man sitting next to me.

"Oh si, señorita, those are for the floods when it rains. Sometimes there is a lot of water and we can't get through."

"And then what?"

"Well, then we just wait, yes. And therefore it is always good to have food and water, because it can take days for the floods to go down. And not many cars travel this road that could help, you know. Si, es muy malo. (Yes, it is very bad.)"

I could not believe what I was hearing. It was a good thing that the rainy season had not started.

Passengers had come and gone. We had stopped in several small towns. They all started to look alike, and I was still in my window seat. A new chauffeur took the wheel to drive us safely through the night.

Very quickly it became dark and it cooled off a little bit. Conversations stopped, radios were packed away and lights turned off. Only the noise of the motor and an occasional snore broke the silence.

I was not tired. A million thoughts crisscrossed my mind. So much had happened in the last few weeks, and now here I was in this bus traveling to Long Beach, California to get married. I could not believe it, but it was true. How lives can change in a short time.

Alberto and I had worked in the same bank in Santiago, Chile, when we began dating. After I changed jobs, we kept seeing each other. This was during a time in Chile when many young people wanted to go to the United States in search of better opportunities, and we were no exception. Alberto's sister had been living in New York for a couple of years by then and was trying to find a sponsor for him, which was all that was needed then for South Americans to get the immigration visa.

In 1960 I had left for the United States to visit friends and was gone for almost four months. I had liked it there and was not opposed to the idea of emigrating in the future. When I returned to Chile, Alberto had joined his sister in New York. We kept in touch by mail.

After a few months in New York, he decided to go to California. He did not like it in New York. Besides, he had found out that a buddy of his from Chile was in the Los Angeles area also. Right after arriving, he knew he liked the West Coast better. The weather and the ocean were to his liking and the people friendlier and more easy going. Now I just had to join him there. Two days before I had flown from Santiago to Mexico City, and, now here I was on this bus en route to Long Beach.

Did I do the right thing? We had very little money and no jobs. How much English did we remember from school? Not much. We had no family or friends in this part of the country to fall back on. Besides, asking for help was out of the question. We were on our own. This made us even more determined to succeed and willing to work hard. I just knew that together we could make it. No doubt, I had made the right choice.

Besides, I wanted to be with him. He was a great guy and fun to be with. He had a wonderful sense of humor and was never short of a comeback. At the same time, he was caring and sensitive to the needs of others, always ready to help. He, too, wanted to take risks, and strive for a better life than he could expect in Chile. To top it off, he was good-looking. He was a littler taller than I, broad-shouldered, with wavy black hair, dark eyes and light olive skin.

With these thoughts, and picturing Alberto in my mind, I fell asleep.

Dawn seemed to come quickly. People were waking up and stretching their stiff bodies. Did we stop somewhere during the night? If we did, I did not notice. I must have been sound asleep. It had not mattered that the hard wooden seats had no reclining backs.

Were we going to have another beautiful day? Through the window I could barely see the outlines of some tall cacti, a few bushes, but not much else. As the horizon became lighter, the sky lit up in all different hues of yellow mixed with a little pink. Then the sun emerged. In only a few minutes, it changed from a very thin curved sliver of light to a full round and bright ball. Nature's show at its best had ended, and a new day was born.

The bus soon stopped in a small village and everybody headed to a cantina they seemed to know very well. I still had my bag of fruit and did not want any coffee.

More towns followed. The bus had fewer passengers now. Not all seats were occupied. I did not mind at all. I had talked to so many people sitting next to me, and had listened to so many of their stories, that a little quiet was welcome. They were just so surprised to have a *gringa* on the bus that they had to satisfy their curiosity.

The hours went by slowly. The desert was never changing. Here and there gusts of wind blew up dirt and debris from the ground, spinning it around and forming small tornados. They were not big enough to cause any harm, just interesting to observe. They seemed to be dancing over the ground and then dissolved into nothing.

The sun had set and it was getting dark. It was not until another couple of hours had passed that the few passengers left on the bus began to collect their belongings from the overhead compartments. We must be getting close to Ciudad Juarez and therefore close to the border, I thought.

The bus stopped in a poorly lit bus terminal. Passengers disembarked and collected their baggage. I, too, got out making sure my two suitcases were still there and hadn't disappeared with somebody else. They were important to me; they were all I had in the way of worldly possessions and I could not afford to lose them. And there they were, the only ones left in that big compartment.

I got on the bus again. Now I was the only passenger left.

Nothing happened. No announcement of any kind had been made previously as to what was scheduled next.

Where is the driver? He had to come back. His jacket was still hanging behind his seat. A few minutes passed. Nothing. Finally he showed up. He grabbed his jacket, a few other things and was just about to leave again, for good.

This cannot be.

"Un momento, señor," I called out as I walked quickly to the front of the bus. The man looked up, startled. I guess he didn't expect anybody to be on the bus.

"Si, señorita, que pasa?

"Well, are we not continuing?"

"No, this is Ciudad Juarez, the last city on our route."

"Well, I don't think so. I am not staying in Ciudad Juarez, you know, I do have a ticket to California and need to be taken across the border to El Paso."

For a minute he just stared at me. Obviously this was not what he wanted to hear.

"Bueno, I'll check with the office and will be back shortly." And without waiting for my answer, he walked off.

He better be back, I thought. This time he had taken his jacket.

The station was deserted by now. All passengers had gone their different ways. A few skeletal stray dogs rummaged through trashcans looking for anything edible. Waves of music came from a distant saloon.

A few minutes passed and I was just about to get off the bus to find some answers when two uniformed men came walking in my direction.

"Buenas noches, señorita. Could I see your ticket, please?"

I pulled it out of my purse again and handed it over. The man smiled politely as he checked it out and gave it back to me.

"No se preocupe (Don't worry), we will take you to El Paso. We just have to wait for a new driver. He will be here shortly. Y perdone la molestia. (Sorry for the inconvenience)."

I was relieved. The prospect of having to stay in this poor border town had not been appealing to me at all, and more so, since it was dark and I didn't know my way around. So this was good news and I did not mind waiting for the driver. They probably had to get an English-speaking one, knowledgeable with border procedures.

It didn't take more than twenty minutes when he appeared. He was a friendly young man, polite, and he appeared to know what he was doing. I moved to the front seat. The road had a lot of potholes, but at least we were going.

"We are not too far from the border now, señorita. It will take us maybe 15 minutes. You will have to get off there. The border patrol will check your documents and then the custom people will take a look at your luggage. The bus depot is right around the corner, where you can get your seat on the next bus to Long Beach."

He unloaded my two suitcases, waived good-by and drove off. A sleepy looking border official glanced at my passport and bus ticket, took one look at my luggage and waved me through. At this time of the night he was in no mood to search anything.

Shortly before daybreak the bus left for Long Beach. What difference in scenery! No more dry and dusty desert. Immense green fields planted with vegetables, alfalfa and other products I could not identify, were visible on both sides of the road. Enormous sprinklers mounted on wheels were irrigating them. The early morning sun made each drop sparkle like little diamonds, a beautiful spectacle in itself. Soon the flat land gave way to hills and rocky mountains covered with gigantic boulders and no vegetation to speak of. The road was steep. To give the bus a rest and the passengers a moment to stretch their legs, we stopped at a lookout. The view was spectacular. What a big country!

The rest of the bus ride was somewhat of a blur of commercial establishments, restaurants and gas stations flying by on the side of the road, all beckoning for business by multicolored neon signs.

"This is Long Beach. Anybody getting off here?" The driver asked.

"I am," I answered as I grabbed my belongings and walked toward the front of the bus. Through the windshield I could see Alberto waiting for me. My heart jumped for joy. I had arrived after 61 hours on the road.

Rhona and Alberto in 1960 in Chile

Alberto Villanueva in 1961

A NEW START IN LONG BEACH

Alberto had rented a furnished apartment on Second Street in Long Beach not too far from where the bus had dropped me off. We both grabbed one of my two suitcases and started walking, talking all the time. There was so much to tell and to catch up on. We had not seen each other in over 7 months. After about 10 blocks we got to an older U-shaped, one-story building with six units on each side and a grassy strip in the middle.

Our apartment was just a single rectangular room with a door to the immediate right leading to the bathroom. Then I saw some large closet doors on that same side and following those was a second door that opened to the kitchen with a built-in nook that served as an eating area. The place had been cleaned the day before. The smell of Lysol was still noticeable in the bathroom.

It had all the basic furniture: a couch, coffee table and a couple of chairs. A big lamp sat on a corner table with room to spare for the telephone. The furniture pieces were used but in good repair. The stuffed couch of a grayish, nondescript color needed some life, but for the time being it was fine. Next to the front door stood a little shelf with some books, old magazines and a vase with plastic red roses. The wall-to-wall carpet was clean. I loved the afternoon sun coming through the big window opposite the front door. It made the room bright and happy.

"This is nice, but do you have to sleep on the couch? There is no bed in this room!" I said as I turned around looking for the missing item.

"Just wait," Alberto answered laughing as he walked to what I thought was a closet and opened the doors. He grabbed the handle of the metal contraption behind it and pulled it down. I was amazed. It was a bed! I had never seen a Murphy bed before. What a clever idea.

The rent was $65 a month and all utilities were included. No last month's rent and no security deposit were required.

For the last six weeks Alberto had been trying to find a permanent job, but so far it was all temporary work. With little English and no practical skills, he was at a disadvantage. Having worked in banking in Chile did not help much. But he was persistent and did not mind taking anything that came along in the meantime. That's how he came to work in construction, setting up a circus tent, cleaning operating rooms in a hospital, unloading tuna at the Starkist Cannery in San Pedro, doing odd jobs at the Texaco refinery, etc. etc. He did not have a car yet, which made it so much harder to get to the different locations having to rely on public transportation. Getting up at about 4:30 in the morning was essential.

The next few days I got acquainted with my surroundings, neighborhood and stores. I found a thrift store where I bought several items for the kitchen for a quarter a piece. A toaster for seventy-five cents just needed a thorough cleaning and worked for many years. A ricer, also for a quarter, I have to this date. And so our new life together began to take shape.

On September 13, 1961, we went to Long Beach City Hall to get married. There were a number of couples with the same idea waiting in line with friends and relatives. Some were wearing wedding dresses and tuxes, others a little less formal and then there were us just in our normal Sunday clothes. One after another they went to the available windows. When done there was a lot of hugging and kissing going on and happiness was in the air.

"Next!" the lady at one of the windows yelled out with a shrill voice.

Our turn. We approached the window with pounding hearts. Luckily, we had all the papers and information she requested. She had to repeat a few questions because we had a hard time understanding but, all in all, it went well. She had us swear with hands held up high that all the information was true and correct. Handing us the marriage license, she congratulated us.

On the way home we bought two gold rings and put them on each other's fingers. We were as happy as we possibly could be.

The next couple of days I kept busy going to the Laundromat, buying a few groceries for dinner, and writing a 13 page long letter to my parents telling them all about my trip, about Long Beach, our apartment and, of course, that we got married on the 13th, my lucky number. That very important piece of paper, our marriage license, was still on the coffee table.

I had looked it over several times but never really taken the time to understand the printed portion, the fine print. Now, since Alberto was at work and I had time, I sat down and read word for word. Our names were clearly on it and spelled correctly. I verified our address and that was fine. But then I saw something I could not understand, something was wrong. How could this have an expiration date!"I don't think we are married" I called out to Alberto the minute he walked in.

"Why do you say that?" he asked, looking at me kind of perplexed.

"This paper has an expiration date? Look at this here." I showed him the particular date on the form.

"Well, I don't know. Why don't you go tomorrow to City Hall and find out. There has to be an explanation." And with that he went to the bathroom to take off his dirty fishy smelling clothes.

Alberto was working at Starkist Tuna now. It was great since workers were allowed to take home some squid, mackerel or other fish caught together with the tuna. Therefore we ate an awful lot of seafood prepared in many different ways. It certainly helped our budget.

The next day, first thing in the morning, I went to City Hall. And, sure enough, this marriage license was more like a permit to get married. I could have fainted. Why didn't the shrill-voiced lady tell us? I guess she must have assumed we knew.

"Come back on the 20th at 11:00 and ask for judge Martin DeVries. He can marry you," the woman behind the counter said.

I rushed home to tell Alberto. I knew that it was too early for him to be back but I was so glad to have the answer to the puzzle. The hours seemed to stand still making it a very long afternoon.

"Well, how did it go? What did you find out?" Alberto asked as he finally came home that evening. I did not need an invitation to speak. The words just poured out of me as I related to him all that was said.

"No problem! We will do as they say and everything will be fine."

We met the judge in his chambers on the 20ᵗʰ as instructed. He was expecting us.

"Do you have a witness?" he asked.

Upon our negative response, he called somebody from the office next door to act as one. We did not care who it was. And then we had to repeat the marriage vows after him. We tried to say it as close as possible to what he said, but we had only a vague idea of what we were saying. Again, we put the rings on each other's finger, kissed and now we were husband and wife. This time we were legal!

A few weeks later, I found out that the long letter to my parents had never arrived in Chile. On one hand I was sad, because my parents had been worried about me, but on the other hand, I was glad because now I could give them the correct marriage date without many explanations.

The following morning promised to be a beautiful warm summer day. The morning fog had already dissipated. We decided to go to the beach just a short walk away. The seagulls were warming themselves in the early morning sun. They stood like soldiers, all facing the same direction with their beaks tucked under their wings.

The water was smooth, hardly any waves, perfect for swimming. Being used to cold waters of the Chile caused by the Humboldt Current running along the coast, we really enjoyed the warmer water temperature.

In the afternoon we went to see the Long Beach pier and the amusement park along the shore. The Pike, as it was called, had many rides, a Ferris wheel, places where to test one's strength and accuracy, shops, hot dog and hamburger stands, BBQ's and fish fry's, whose aromas floated in the air and opened people's appetites, and of course the big roller coaster.

"Do you want to go for a ride on this one?" Alberto asked not really waiting for my answer but walking toward the ticket kiosk to pay for the admittance.

The line advanced slowly and then it was our turn to take a seat. A metal bar across our laps locked us in and then we went up, up and even further up. The first plunge down almost took my breath away. By the time I came to my senses we were ready for the next descent into an abyss. After several repeats of this up and down we came to a standstill. The metal bar clicked open and we got out. I was shaking and my legs were wobbly. That was my first and last ride on a roller coaster. And to think we had to pay for this!

Across from the Pike on the other side of Ocean Boulevard was an old section of Long Beach frequented mostly by sailors. It showed signs of neglect. We walked along the street and saw many bars, tattoo places, a movie theater, rundown hotels, and pawn shops. Every so often a whiff of stale beer and tobacco smoke emerged from these establishments and loud music tried to cover it all up. Old people sat on benches along the street and in the small lobbies of the hotels. Their faces showed hopelessness and boredom. They were just lonely people with nothing to look forward to. Very sad! It was not an area we wanted to come back to.

We loved Belmont Shores with its vitality and hustle and bustle. Even in the evenings people strolled along the sidewalks window-shopping, eating an ice cream or just hanging out with friends; whereas in other neighborhoods, there was not a soul to be seen after dark.

I started working in a preschool nursery for children afflicted with cerebral palsy. It was located next to the Long Beach Community Hospital. My job was to help out wherever needed with twelve two-year olds. Some toddlers sat in wheelchairs, others could crawl or walk. It was like a big household with mealtimes, naps, snacks, educational toys, group activities and physical therapy. All wanted attention and tender loving care. After everybody had left, I had to clean the place.

With the extra income we decided to buy a black and white television. We needed more exposure to the English language and wanted to keep up with the world events. It was the only luxury we indulged in. Not that it was very fancy. It was just a black metal box with rabbit ears as antenna and the legs could be screwed off and on, which made it easy to transport.

Then, a new hurdle presented itself. We needed to establish "credit." This was a new concept for us. We were used to paying cash for everything we bought as we did with the television set. Somewhere down the road we needed a car. Maybe we could buy one sooner and pay later.

"Lets go to Bank of America and ask for a loan" I asked Alberto assuring him that we would not spend the money. "We have both steady jobs now and it can't hurt to find out. Besides we have already a checking account with them."

The loan officer at the Bank took down our information. We had brought the last pay slips, our green cards and passports.

"How much do you want, and what do you need the money for?" the man asked.

"We would like about $500 to buy some furniture. We want to move to an unfurnished apartment to save money."

"That makes sense. You can have up to $600, and we can set it up right now."

We could not believe it! He is actually giving us the money and he doesn't even know us!

"That would be wonderful! And we would like to open a Savings account at the same time to leave the money there until we need it," I replied as I squeezed Alberto's hand under the table.

"Of course, that is not a problem." We received the money, deposited it in the savings account and made the loan payments for less than a year before paying it off completely. That was the beginning of our "credit".

After about six months we decided to buy a car and to look for a bigger apartment. We needed transportation to give us more flexibility and freedom. The car turned out to be a four-year old Ford Fairlane, light blue and white, with white wall tires. It was out of this world, so beautiful and cost us a fortune: $1,300. The monthly payments were steep but affordable and we intended to pay it off as soon as possible. Back in Chile only a well-to-do person could afford a car like this and we had one in less than a year! We were ecstatic!

With the newly acquired mobility, we found a second-story one-bedroom apartment on Ximeno and Second Street close to Belmont Shore. We did not have to pay more than the $65 we were paying now, had more room, but it was unfurnished. We took it.

At garage sales we found a bed, a kitchen table with a brown Formica top and six chairs with metal legs typical of the fifties and sixties, two small upholstered chairs for the living room and a couple of lamps. An old sofa bed was given to us as well as a coffee table. The thrift shop supplied us with more small household items. Linens and towels came from Sears. Those I wanted to be new.

We were set at very little cost. We were making progress and happy to have made the move to this country.

Ford Fairlane

XIMENO

It was a beautiful summer in 1962, and we took full advantage of it. Lots of our free time was spent at the beach basking in the sun, trying to get that perfect tan. In those days, nobody knew about damaging ultraviolet rays and the consequences of overexposure to the sun. We just tried not to burn by applying lots of suntan lotion. We made a trip to San Francisco along marvelous Highway 1. The scenery was breathtaking. After every curve a new panorama presented itself; secluded coves and sandy beaches way down below the road, too steep to reach; stretches of rocky coastline with big waves crashing against it, throwing the water like geysers high into the air and then receding as if nothing had happened. It was a constant free show of nature.

Many afternoons we drove around getting to know Long Beach and the surrounding areas. We visited Marineland with its many aquariums and varieties of sea life. It was like a marine museum, a heaven for scientists.

For us it was a time of adventure and exploration, and adaptation to our life in the United States. Even though the climate and vegetation were the same as in the central part of Chile, the daily life was somewhat different. Much to our delight, we ate dinner early and not at 10 o'clock at night.

At the beginning I could not get over the waste of many things. I was used to bringing my own cloth shopping bags to bring groceries home in. Here I was given paper bags that later were thrown away! All those glass jars and bottles, small and large, filled with different products, also got dumped. They would have been wonderful containers for something else in Chile. At the weekly farmers market in Long Beach, I was pleasantly surprised, though. I could select my own fruit and vegetables! In Chile the vendor did that for you and invariably threw in a bad one he wanted to get rid of.

We adapted quickly. Why stick to the old ways when the new ones were better, and here they were better, more advanced and more practical.

It was mid-October now and some alarming news was transmitted over the radio.

"Did you hear something about nuclear missiles in Cuba?" I asked Alberto after he came home from work. "This is kind of dangerous being so close to the United States mainland, don't you think? I hope it does not turn ugly." Alberto had not given it much thought, having worked all day, but that evening we were glued to the television, listening to the commentators. We learned about the disaster at the Bay of Pigs and Kruschev's promise to help Castro defend Cuba against America. They showed pictures taken by spy-planes of missile bases in Cuba.

A few days later a U2 plane was shot down over Cuba. It looked as if war was about to happen.

All this made me very nervous. I did not want to go through another war. Besides, a year ago, Alberto had to register with the Selective Service; it was mandatory. He was given number 4-128-31-280, and could possibly be called in for active duty. My imagination took enormous proportions! Going to work was a good distraction.

The Cuban Missile Crisis lasted about two weeks. People were getting hysterical and started to horde non-perishable foods and liquids. Grocery stores were out of canned goods and bottled juices.

Finally, President Kennedy and Kruschev came to an agreement: the American blockade of Cuba was to be lifted and the Russian planes and ships would return to Russia. The crisis was over. Both sides had had a fright, which translated into the start of the end of the Cold War.

Life was good again with everything back to normal.

Christmas came and went and on March 17, 1963, our baby daughter was born. What a life-changing event! Anabelle was the center of attention now and we were very proud parents. Many times a day I stood by her crib watching her sleep in her baby sweaters I had knitted and on the sheets I had embroidered with baby motifs. We were so lucky and happy to have this little baby. I had quit my job and now was a full-time mom. It was a time of trial and error with no other female advice around but we did just fine. She was healthy and growing and walked at nine months. With gasoline purchases we had accumulated Blue Chip stamps and were able to get a stroller. Our budget was somewhat tighter now since I was not working, but we managed.

After summer vacation I received a call from the director of the preschool nursery where I had worked, asking if I wanted to come back on a part time basis. I agreed. I found a babysitter on the next block. She seemed nice and also had a six- months-old daughter. I went to work and was miserable the whole day. It was a big mistake. I just could not do this. I missed her too much and was worried. It was not worth the fifteen dollars a week I would take home after paying the sitter. And that was the end of my working days for quite a few years.

At the beginning of 1964, knowing that we would have another baby at the end of April, we decided to make a big move. We wanted to buy a small house. It was a daring idea, and we thought it over and over. The money we spent on rent was wasted, with no benefit to us. It was better to apply it toward a mortgage on a house. Besides, we did not want to stay in that apartment forever with two small children. They needed room to play.

The opportunity presented itself sooner than expected. It was an older two bedroom, one bath house on raised foundations in North Long Beach on Rose Street selling for $13,900 and the monthly mortgage payments would be $96. The exterior had a fresh coat of paint and the rest needed some tender loving care and sprucing up but nothing major. A one-car garage was in the back of the deep lot with an old asphalt driveway leading to it. One big problem: We did not have the down payment of $500, nor the money for the closing costs which were $200. This had all come so quick, and we did not have the sufficient time to save some money. But we had two good friends willing to help us out. The $200 we promised Hector Palaziol to pay back as soon as possible and sealed the deal with a handshake. Hector was Alberto's co-worker who had immigrated to the United States from Argentina a few years earlier. For the $500 we signed a note and a second trust deed to Pat and Ze Alves Da Silva. We had met them when I was working at Tichenors, the preschool nursery. Their Daughter Lisa was enrolled there and we had been friends ever since.

Luckily the car was paid off by then, and we did not have any other debts.

Was this a dream or something? We were stunned. Could this be that in a few weeks we would be the owners of a house, no matter how small? Two and half years earlier we paid the rent of our first apartment, which left us with only two hundred dollars in our pockets and no steady jobs and little knowledge of the English language. And now this!

Only in America!

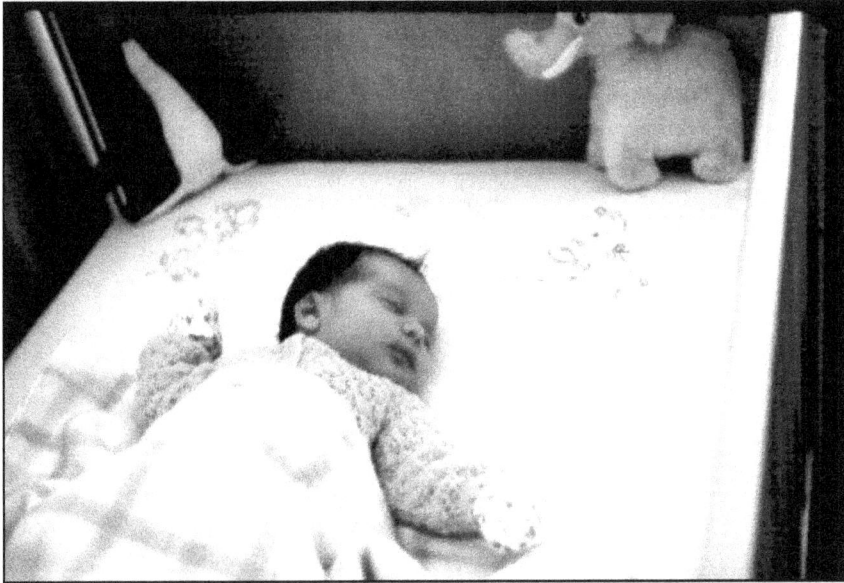

Anabelle Patricia Villanueva

170

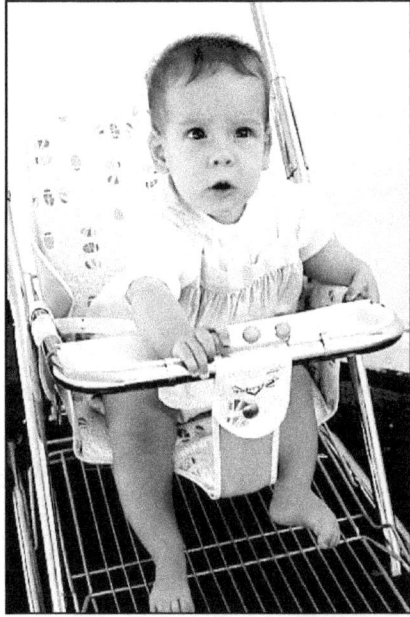

Anabelle's first birthday

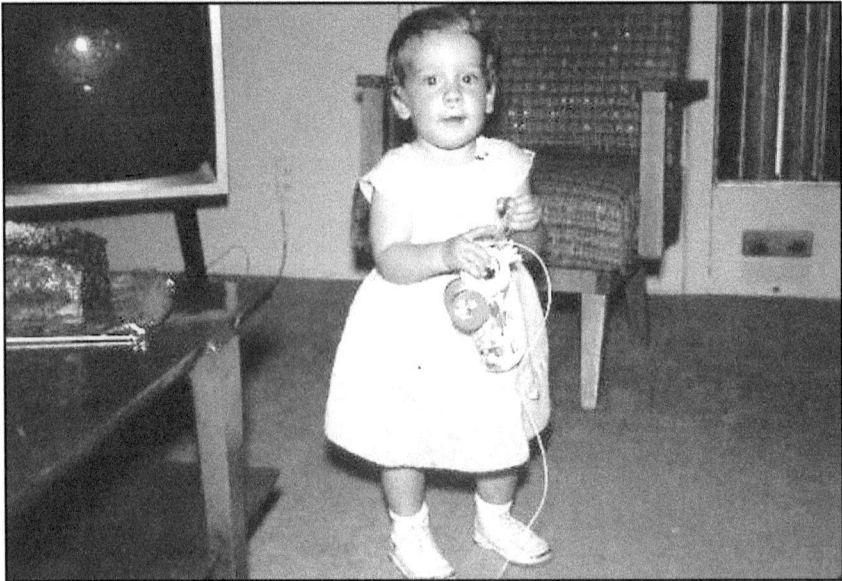

"Here are the keys to your house. You can move in any time you want," Helen, our real estate lady, called out as she stepped into our apartment. "Escrow closed this morning and it is all yours." We gave her a big hug and thanked her for all her help to make this possible. She was just as excited as we were, and right away we made plans for the move.

"I think I can get the truck from work. We can move everything with ease in one weekend." Alberto said. "I will ask Hector to help us with the furniture."

"I can have all the kitchen stuff boxed up, and the bedding and clothes as well," I said, figuring in my head how many boxes were needed. "And I will clean the house before moving in."

"I will bring some pizza and beer for lunch on Saturday, so you don't have to worry about food," Helen added, laughing.

The next couple of weeks went by quickly, yet not quick enough for us. We just couldn't wait to move, even though we had been very happy in this apartment.

Alberto was given the permission to take the truck for a weekend. He had been working for this new company for approximately six months now. With the recommendation of Ze Alves da Silva, our Portuguese friend, Alberto had been hired to work in the warehouse of Korody-Colyer Corporation, a company that made replacement parts for diesel engines. Ze was in charge of the export department. It was a small privately owned business with only about twenty employees, primarily immigrants from countries like Hungary, Chile, Argentina, Portugal, Germany, Italy, and Mexico. All were working together peacefully trying to get ahead in life.

Our move went smoothly. Only two trips were needed, since our possessions consisted only of the most essential items. By the end of the weekend, all the furniture pieces were in their place, boxes emptied and contents put away. During those couple of days, little Anabelle was safe in her wooden playpen in the kitchen. She watched us with big eyes, never having seen such commotion, so much going back and forth.

The house was small. Through the front door one entered the rectangular living room to the right. On the far end of the left wall, a door opened to the kitchen. Opposite the front entrance was another door leading to a small hallway, the middle of the house. The two bedrooms were in the back, and the bathroom was squeezed in between the kitchen and the left bedroom. The floors were hardwood, except for the kitchen and the bathroom, which were beige linoleum. The kitchen had a very convenient side entrance from the driveway, which we used daily. All rooms had at least a couple of windows, which made it light and airy. The smell of fresh paint and Lysol still lingered in the air.

The front and back yards were in a sad state. The house had been vacant for several months and nobody had bothered to water the grass and the few bushes and trees. I did not mind. Plans were already forming in my head as to how to make this garden blossom.

It was an old, somewhat neglected house but for us it was our castle.

Six weeks later, on April 26, 1964, our baby boy, Alan, made our family complete. He was a very good baby, just as Anabelle had been. They hardly ever cried. Clean diapers and full tummies contributed greatly to that. I was a very busy mom now with two small children just 13 months apart. Twice a week I went to the laundromat with about four-to five-dozen diapers. The disposable ones had just come on the market but were too expensive for us.

With spring in full force, the grass began to grow, as well as all the weeds in the cracks of the old asphalt driveway. It looked terrible! Alberto again borrowed the truck and began to remove the asphalt. It was back-breaking labor. He then took the heavy loads to the free dump on Bonita Canyon Road in what was to become the city of Newport Coast with multi-million dollar homes. A few weeks later a construction company came and poured a new cement driveway for $300. It looked beautiful. What an improvement!

All this time Alberto had taken any additional jobs he could find to make extra money. This way we paid Hector Palaciol the $200 we owed him, acquired a new driveway, and now our new goal was a much-needed washing machine. Alberto also had a new project: a new wide gate over the driveway, closing off access to the backyard.

The following summer months we spent mostly at home. We were happy just being together in the back yard, and there was always something to do or fix around the house. On hot days I turned on a sprinkler and Anabelle had fun running through the water. Alan slept peacefully in the shade in a small portable bed. The flowers I had planted were blooming and their fragrance could be smelled throughout the yard. Flowering jasmine clung to the wooden fence by wrapping their tentacles around the boards. Often we picnicked outside. It was so peaceful.

Fall and winter came. The house was getting cold and we started to use the old wall heater. One morning someone knocked at the door. It was our next-door neighbor.

"Do you know you have sparks flying out of your heater vent on the roof? That is dangerous," she said as we all went outside to take a look. Sure enough, the sparks looked like swarms of fireflies. Needless to say, we turned the heater off.

The next day I tried to call a repairman but had trouble with our party-line phone. The other people were constantly talking. Finally I was able to make an appointment.

He was very punctual, took a look at the heater and said that he had to go under the house to see what was wrong. Then he started to mumble down below, and it was getting louder and louder, but I could not understand a word he was saying. I waved to my neighbor, who happened to be in the front yard, to come over.

"What is going on down there? Can you understand him?" I asked when she entered the kitchen.

She listened for a few minutes and started to laugh. "You don't want to know what he is saying. He is frustrated and using four-letter-words that would make a sailor blush."

As the swearing down below continued, I also had to laugh. Sometimes it is good not to understand the language.

Shortly after, the man emerged from below the house through the crawlspace. "Lady, you have all sorts of bugs and creepy crawlers down there," he said, as he went outside to shake off the dirt from his overalls. "I cleaned the heater and made the necessary adjustments, but eventually it needs to be replaced, "he said, wiping his dirty hands on his pants.

That was not good news. From then on we used the heater as little as possible because we couldn't afford to replace it just then.

It was Christmas Eve, our first in this little house. I had bought a small Douglas fir for $2.50, and made it festive with decorations and lights I had from previous years. Unwrapped toys were arranged on the floor around the tree. I remembered the happiness of the Christmas after the war in Germany in 1946, when the door opened and I saw the beautiful tree. I wanted our little family to be just as happy now.

The scent of the green tree filled the house. In the kitchen the aroma of freshly baked cookies still lingered in the air.

After dark we opened the door to the living room. At first the children were quiet, taking in the sight, not knowing what to think of it. Then Anabelle and Alan discovered the toys and the excitement showed on their faces. Anabelle ran over to inspect the gifts and Alan crawled quickly after her. They played all evening as we watched and sipped our homemade eggnog. Life was good!

Alan 6 weeks old and Anabelle 15 month

Sisterly love

Fun in the back yard

Alan Villanueva

Ready for an outing

Anabelle loves Daddy

ON THE MOVE AGAIN

"How about selling your house and moving into something bigger and newer?" Helen, our friend and real estate agent, asked us one day in late 1965. "You have been in this one for over eighteen months now. Prices have gone up and you improved this property. You could clear about $2500, which could be used for a down payment."

This was something to think about. She was right. We had put in the long driveway to the garage in the back of the property. The pretty white fence with a wide gate was finished. We had painted the house inside and out and made a few needed repairs. The front and back yards were well taken care of and I had planted many flowers. It looked much nicer now then when we moved in.

Should we consider a move or were we going too fast and taking a big risk?

Many tract homes were being built in Orange County. It was further away from Alberto's workplace, but prices were lower. We started to look around to get some ideas about what was being offered. All the model homes were professionally decorated and landscaped and looked so attractive. I would like this or that I thought many times when we went through them. Indeed, maybe we should sell the house and move. It was a constant back and forth. It would be nice to have an attached two-car garage with a place for a washer and dryer. But could we afford it?

After many discussions, calculations, possible alternatives, and sleepless nights, we decided to go ahead and sell.

Within three weeks we had an offer for $17,000, which we accepted.

We rented a two-bedroom apartment in Anaheim and lived there for a few months, meanwhile we looked for a house to buy. The apartment was quite pleasant. It had a small, enclosed patio where the children could play. In walking distance was a grammar school with a playground equipped with slides, swings and monkey bars. Nearby Knott's Berry Farm also kept us entertained. It was free then, and we spent many Saturdays or Sundays there.

At the beginning of 1966, we finally found a house in the Westmont Tract of Fountain Valley, close to Warner and Bushard streets. It was only a little over a year old, with three bedrooms, two baths, living room and a large kitchen and family room combination. A staircase led from the family room to the upstairs unfinished "bonus room". The bonus room alone was the size of a two-car garage. All the rafters and two-by-fours were exposed, as well as the plumbing for a possible future bathroom. The owners could finish it according to their own design. The location of the house was not too far from the 405 Freeway, which at that time ended at Beach Blvd. A grammar school was just across the street and the high school, also in walking distance, had just been finished. The surrounding area was quite rural, with many vegetable and strawberry fields. A bike ride to the beach was uninterrupted by traffic signals. The Fountain Valley Post Office had just started to deliver the mail, which was a big help for the people living in the area.

We liked it and asked Helen to present an offer of $26,000, with 10% down and a second trust deed note of $2,600.

We had waited a couple of days when Helen called to tell us that she was coming by our place.

"You got yourselves a new house," Helen exclaimed as she walked into our apartment. "They accepted the offer and we can close escrow in about three weeks. In a few days I will bring all the paperwork to be signed. I don't foresee any problems in getting a five percent loan, and to make it easier for you, I will waive half of my commission."

"But Helen, you are doing all this work and it takes time. We can't accept that."

"Oh, yes you can. You have been working hard, you are good folks and you deserve a break."

We were stunned. As we expressed our gratitude, she just waved us off and said "start packing." That we did.

It was a real shock to move from a small apartment to this for us giant 1800-square- foot house. We sat on the couch, looked around and could not believe that this was ours. Now we just had to make the payments, which were $210 a month, taxes included. Alberto was bringing home only $360. That made me very nervous, and the first week I cried a lot.

"Don't worry so much." Alberto told me several times when he saw me downcast and serious. "We will be fine. Once we pay off the second trust deed, it will be easy to make the payments on the first."

"Well, I hope you are right," I responded. I was scared, but then my common sense took over. As I was unpacking the boxes I thought that I could also work and earn some money if needed and that idea helped chase away my fears.

With packing, moving, unpacking and settling into the new surroundings, we didn't have a chance to celebrate Anabelle's third birthday in March. And since Alan was turning two in a couple of weeks, we decided to celebrate both birthdays together. I baked a chocolate cake and bought each of them a toy at the old TG&Y store. We sang "Happy Birthday to You" and lit the candles, three on one side of the cake and two on the other. The kids' eyes lit up and they were eager to blow them out, not only once but several times. They were happy, and so were Alberto and I. Now, with this little celebration, the house had really become our home.

A few months later I started to babysit other kids. Usually I had two or three, sometimes even four preschoolers from the neighborhood, plus our own two. It was like a mini kindergarten. They all played well together and had fun. I didn't have very many toys by today's standards, so I made some out of card board boxes. They loved to hide in them or play house. I improvised a lot. Nap time after lunch was something I looked forward to. Maybe, just maybe I would have a few moments of peace and quiet, time to recharge.

With the extra income of $15 per child per week, we began the big project of finishing the upstairs room. We wanted to make it into a family room with a half-bath so guests could stay there also. With city permits in hand and lots of good advice from the people at the now defunct National Lumber Company, we went ahead with this new project. Every Saturday we bought a few sheets of drywall and rolls of fiberglass insulation. It was hard work and we were learning. It took us many weeks but, eventually, the last piece of drywall and paneling was nailed in.

A plumber made the necessary connections to install the toilet and the washbasin. The banister along the top of the staircase was beautiful and Alberto was very proud of this, his first woodworking project.

We were amazed by the progress we had made in our lives and were proud of it. In five years we went from arriving in California almost penniless, with no job offers, and little knowledge of the English language, to this roomy house. To make it even better, we were debt free, except for the mortgage on the house.

18784 Olive St., Fountain Valley, Ca.92708

FOUNTAIN VALLEY

Life in Fountain Valley, a small city then, was good. We were happy there. We knew our neighbors, the children played together, and we felt secure. Many times we left the door to our house unlocked without worrying. Nothing was going to happen. The children watched "Casper the Friendly Ghost", "Captain Kangaroo", "Sesame Street", "Lassy", "Flipper" and later "I Love Lucy", "Happy Days" with the Fonz, "Bonanza" and "Bewitched". They were all programs without violence, where the good guy always won. Life was simple and uncomplicated.

Whenever a Walt Disney movie was shown at the Fountain Valley Drive-In Theater on Brookhurst Street, we packed the station wagon with blankets and pillows for Anabelle and Alan, and spent an evening there with the loud speaker hooked onto the car window.

Alberto's work had improved also. He was not working in the warehouse of Korody-Colyer anymore. After about one year they had transferred him to the office and increased his salary.

"Guess who is coming to visit from Chile?" I asked Alberto one day when he was coming home from work and getting out of the car.

"Who?"

"My mom!"

"Is that so. How long is she going to stay?" Alberto asked as he was taking off his shoes to go into the house.

"Just a few weeks and then she'll fly back to Chile."

I was so excited about the prospect of having her here. There was so much to talk about. She would have the latest news from Chile. My aunt Rita was not a very good letter writer, her mail came very sporadically.

I was so very glad that Mom was making this trip. She had worked so hard all these years and deserved a vacation.

Once she got over the jet-lag we did a lot of sightseeing with her, which was fun for all of us. We visited Disneyland, the now demolished Marineland in San

Pedro, and Knott's Berry Farm. We went for a weekend to Las Vegas leaving the kids with friends, a first for us and a little distressing for me, but all went well.

Another time we went up north to show her the majestic redwoods and came back along the coast on beautiful Highway 1. She loved it all.

The weeks of her visit with us just flew by and in no time she had to leave again. I think it was hard for her to return to Chile and leave us behind. She had enjoyed her grandkids and would miss them. Life is very hard sometimes.

A couple of years later during the summer Imme came to visit us. We had gone to school together in Chile and had been friends ever since.

She was born in Valparaiso to German parents, had twin brothers and one sister and knew so many people. Besides, she had stayed in touch with all the other classmates in Chile and now could tell me all about them. We did all the touristy things with her and years later we still remembered the many Marie Callender's strawberry pies we ate during her stay. It was her favorite desert.

She loved it here. She loved it so much that she put an ad in the local German weekly newspaper looking for a job. Two parties contacted her and one offered her work in an office. With that job offer in hand, she returned to Chile to apply for an immigration visa. In 1969 she was back to stay and, just like us, not once did she regret that decision.

In the meantime Dad, being a ham-operator, had established a link to us via another ham-operator in Barstow who called me on the phone and then switched us back and forth when he heard one of us say "over". This way we could communicate in a very affordable way. Telephone calls to Chile were very expensive, close to three dollars a minute.

In the early 1970s, dad began to complain that the egg business was deteriorating in Chile. Big enterprises had sprung up with 50,000 hens or more. It was difficult for small outfits to compete.

"We are still doing ok, but I don't know for how long," dad said. "We are doing much of the work ourselves and have kept only one worker, Sergio. To make matters worse, the cost of chicken feed is skyrocketing."

In another one of these conversations I found out that Marxist Salvador Allende was running for president. This was his fourth try. Would he succeed? I was worried.

"You know what, I am going to apply for the U.S. citizenship." I told Alberto one day. "We have been here long enough, and, as it is, we are here to stay."

"What brought that up?" he asked, perplexed.

"Well, what if Allende becomes president? I just want to be prepared in case we have to bring my parents over here. As a citizen I could request them without any problem."

"So do it. The process takes about three months, at least that's what it took when I did it."

I applied, studied the little booklet I was given, passed my test, and took the oath in Santa Ana's City Hall among hundreds of other candidates.

Just in case they were needed, I sent all the necessary papers to Mom and Dad so they could request an immigration visa to the United States. We wanted them to join us in California to get away from political turmoil and financial difficulties. It was a hard decision for them since it meant another new beginning in a different country. In the end, they agreed. They filled out all the forms they were given at the U.S. Embassy and submitted them shortly thereafter for processing.

I was happy I could do that for them and maybe we could be reunited.

Then we received the devastating news.

On September 4, 1970 Salvador Allende won the presidency in Chile. He was the first Marxist leader of a nation to gain the presidency through democratic process. Upon assuming power, he began to carry out his platform of implementing socialistic programs in Chile.

He nationalized large-scale industries, copper mines and banks. Large farms were seized and distributed among the workers who did not have the capital or the know-how to cultivate the land, thereby losing years of crops. He froze prices while raising salaries several times. Lack of food staples produced a black market. Copper, Chile's single most important export, experienced a sharp decline in price on the world market. Chile was drifting toward bankruptcy.

Allende re-established diplomatic relations with Cuba. Shortly after, Fidel Castro made a month-long visit to Chile. He held massive rallies in the National Soccer Stadium lasting many hours each, and gave advice to Allende.

Law and order became non-existent. Bands of Marxist agitators seized private homes at gunpoint and forced people to leave. There was no authority to turn to for complaints. Many Chilean citizens and most foreigners were leaving the country, not wanting to live under a Marxist regime.

Dad organized a large group of neighbors who for months drove through their streets at night to prevent seizure of their properties. On their rounds they kept in touch with walky-talkies. All were armed, ready to shoot.

October 1972 saw the first of what were to be confrontational strikes. The 24-day trucker strike paralyzed the country. The owners, who feared requisitioning of their vehicles, hid the trucks. Inflation of close to one thousand percent had plunged the country into chaos. People stood in lines for hours to get the most basic staples like flour, sugar, oil and some vegetables and fruit. Store shelves were empty. The country now was practically bankrupt. The Allende government then announced it would default on debts to international creditors and foreign governments.

At the beginning of 1973, General Augusto Pinochet was made Commander-in-Chief of the Army and rumors of a possible coup emerged. Private citizens urged the police and armed forces to do something to remedy this situation. On the streets people approached policemen or any soldiers walking about and appealed to their valor and their sense of responsibility toward the people. When that did not work, they accused them of cowardice.

On September 11, 1973, Chile was finally taken over by the military. Just prior to the capture of La Moneda (the Presidential Palace in Santiago) Allende committed suicide with an automatic rifle given to him by Fidel Castro as a gift, which had a golden plate engraved "To my good friend Salvador from Fidel."

As this was occurring and to make matters worse, the unexpected happened: Mom became ill early 1973. After doctor visits, examinations and tests were done, she had a small cancerous part of her bladder removed. Doctors were very optimistic about the outcome and let her go home to recuperate in her familiar surroundings.

After a few months at home, Mom felt bad again. One of her kidneys was so badly infected that it had to be taken out. She never came home again. The cancer had spread. Modern day treatments for cancer were unknown then, and on September 15, 1973, four days after the military takeover, she passed away at the age of 63.

Mom was buried in Santiago in her brother's cemetery plot. It was not possible to bring her to Malloco due to the military coup, road closures and general confusion.

A few weeks before her death I had wanted to fly to Chile.

"Dad, I can fly next Monday and be there Tuesday morning."

"I know you want to come but please don't. The situation here is extremely unstable. Besides, your mother is heavily sedated and would not be aware of your presence."

"Is the political situation really so bad?"

"Yes, and it is getting worse every day."

"But I would like to see Mom."

"I know, I know, believe me, but please stay home and don't come," he pleaded. "The situation here is about to explode. I don't want you to be affected by this. You being here would be another worry more for me. I have too much on my plate already."

And so I did not travel until three months later.

Then I saw the devastation of the Allende Government. Shops were empty, the shelves bare. Graffiti and political slogans were painted on every wall. Beggars sat at every corner with their bent up tin cups.

When the military junta took over, the situation slowly began to improve. Over the years Inflation was brought down to normal levels. A subway system was built in Santiago, social security was implemented and infrastructure improved. Some of the confiscated properties and businesses were returned to their rightful owners. Over the years Santiago was transformed into a modern city and the country prospered.

Dad managed to hang on to the business for a few more years. When the expenses overtook the income, he started selling all the hens, then the truck and, little by little, all the other now unnecessary equipment. Those sales were his only income. With non-existing health insurance his savings had been depleted during Mom's illness.

On December 1, 1984 he died of heart failure at the age of 75.

When I got the call, within hours I flew to Chile to arrive just in time for the funeral. He was buried in Malloco. Twenty years later, when I visited Chile, I also went to Malloco and the cemetery. I could tell that someone was taking care of the grave because it was planted with flowers. That showed that he had many friends among the people in that little village.

But for the rest of my life, I will not forgive myself for not having brought him to California. After Mom's death, he did not want to come anymore, but more than anything else, he did not want to be a burden to us. I should have insisted more and just maybe he would have changed his mind.

We lived in Fountain Valley for eighteen years. Anabelle and Alan went to Nieblas Elementary School across the street and then moved on to Fountain Valley High, also within walking distance. In about 1971 I had stopped babysitting. Toddlers did not fit into our household anymore. The activities of our growing children had changed and they were no longer compatible with those of the younger ones. In 1974 I took a job in a bank five minutes from home. We had bought a Van and I wanted to pay it off early. In the end that job was to last 25 years.

It was a comfortable house and we probably would still be living there had it not been for the growth of the city and the subsequent elevated street noise. Our house was backing up to Bushard Street and traffic noise had increased tremendously. The 405 Freeway had been extended further south from Beach Boulevard and now was too close to us. People said the noise sounded like the waves of the ocean but we could not see the similarity.

In 1984 we moved to our current house in Huntington Beach and we don't have any intention to move again.

Anabelle, Mom, and Alan

Anabelle, Mom and Alan in 1967

Mom and Dad in the early fifties

Dad at 75, six month before his death

VISITING ESTONIA IN 2004

The airplane sat on the runway in the hot midday sun, its engines roaring, ready for take off. Pressed against the back of our seats, we lifted off and were in the air with the blue ocean below us. Our destination was Tallinn, Estonia, the city where I was born.

Having left that country at age five, I didn't remember anything about my birthplace. What I knew of our life in Estonia came from my parent's conversations and the precious photographs they had carefully saved over the years. Would I recognize some of those buildings? Everything must have changed after sixty-five years.

At the Tallinn airport we were greeted by Toivo Kitvel, a man we had never met personally. All we knew was that he was a retired university professor very much interested in the beginning of Estonian aviation, and that he had written two books about the subject.

Eighteen months earlier, when he was gathering material for his second book, Toivo searched the Internet for information about my dad. He found my twenty-year younger cousin, Ulrich Brasche, residing in Germany, who directed his request to my aunt in England. She, being twelve years younger than my dad and not knowing much about Dad's activities in Estonia, sent the letter to me. And thus began an intense correspondence via e-mail.

"Look, there is that tall, dark-haired man in jeans holding a sign. See, it says 'Hola, I am Toivo.' That's him. Let's go to meet him," I exclaimed excitedly as I grabbed my bags and motioned for Alberto to follow me.

"Hello, I think we are the ones you are looking for" I said, as I shook his hand. "I am Rhona and this is Alberto, my husband."

"Welcome to Estonia!" he replied as he handed me a small bunch of flowers, an Estonian custom as I found out later. As we walked toward the exit he laid out his plan for the day. "I will take you to your hotel so you can rest a little. In a couple of hours I will pick you up for some sightseeing, if that is ok with you. The wind will have diminished by then, but do dress warm."

The hotel was under Russian management. It was an old building, but the room was clean and we had our own bathroom. Communicating was difficult since only one lady spoke a little English and she was not always there.

"Toivo seems to be a nice fellow, and tall, at least six feet four or five inches," I said as we were resting on our beds.

"Yes, and he can talk fast too! Did you hear him when he was speaking with the taxi driver?" Alberto commented, "They had a lot to say to each other."

"It always sounds faster when one doesn't understand the language. I just know that he spoke in Russian," I replied as I turned on my side on the squeaky bed. "He is also fluent in Finnish, speaks some German and Spanish, and, of course, Estonian. We always e-mailed in English, though. It's amazing!"

"We better go downstairs, we don't want to make him wait," Alberto said a while later as he put his jacket on. "Don't forget your camera."

Toivo took us to the old part of town situated on a small hill called Toompea. A massive wall complete with eighteen watchtowers surrounded this area. The stone castle stood on the highest part. These were the well-preserved remnants of the fortification dating back to the thirteenth century when Tallinn belonged to the Hanseatic League.

We walked through the main streets and marveled at the sight of elaborately decorated entrances and facades of the medieval buildings then belonging to various guilds and brotherhoods. Toivo also pointed out a pharmacy that was in operation since 1422.

We continued along quaint narrow cobblestone streets past the old German school, now housing a dance studio, and then reached the German Dome Church, the oldest building of the Big Fortress. The church was built in 1229 by Danish monks, then burned down in 1684 together with most of the buildings on Toompea. It was rebuilt soon after and has been in use ever since. It is a small church whose walls and pylons were covered with coats of arms of 107 noble families.

It was overwhelming for me to see these places with my own eyes after having heard so much talk about them when I was younger. I felt like I had made my first real connection with Estonia!

A couple of days later we took our luggage to Toivo's house. He had an old "Volga," a Russian car. It was on its last legs but managed to hold up during our four-day excursion with Toivo as driver and translator. Our destination was Kullamaa, about 35 miles southwest of Tallinn, the place where my father was born. Would I recognize the house with the thickly thatched roof and the church nearby? I was not sure.

It was a very relaxing drive, with hardly any traffic, and the scenery was beautiful. Birch trees lined the road. Woods alternated with freshly plowed fields, where long-legged storks looked for food. Small houses dotted the landscape. The bright sunshine gave it all a happy face.

As we drove into Kullamaa, I was on the lookout. Where was it?

"I know of one church. We are almost there. Maybe it is the one we are looking for," Toivo said, as he entered a wide dirt road to the left. From the distance we saw a steeple poking out of the treetops. As we came closer, we saw the church building on a corner and a newer house across the street.

"Wait, stop," I exclaimed excitedly. "Do you see the building in the back on the same side as the church? I think this is it. I am almost positive. Let's go and take a look."

As we got out of the car, walked past the church and on toward the house, I knew I was right. This was the place where my grandparents had lived and where my father was born. The original thatched roof was no longer there; an ugly gray-colored metal one had replaced it. Windowpanes were broken. It looked abandoned. Still, I knew I was right.

"Let's see if we can find somebody who could show us around," Toivo said, as he walked back toward the newer house across from the church. A man opened the door. As it turned out he was the pastor who had just returned from a business trip. Toivo introduced us and explained the reasons why we were here. The man's face lit up and he immediately offered to open the church as well as the old house.

It was a plain gothic Lutheran church. The wooden pews were antiques but in good repair. There was nothing that could distract someone from listening to a sermon. No pictures, no statues. It must have looked just like that, when my grandfather left in 1932, with one exception: there was a microphone on the pulpit.

Next to the church was an old overgrown cemetery. One small section was fenced in and well kept. Yellow flowers were growing; the ground was raked. Then I saw the names. Those were the graves of my dad's four younger brothers and sisters who died as infants, and one brother who succumbed to blood poisoning at age nineteen. I gasped and tried to hold back my tears. What a shock! The emotions and memories overwhelmed me. I had not expected to see that.

As we walked to the old house the pastor informed us that the large home had been converted into a hospital during Russian occupation. In later years it was partially occupied by a doctor's practice and now, after being vacant for several years and in need of extensive repair, it was returned to the parish. Russians use, but don't maintain, much less repair.

Upon returning to the pastor's house he invited us in for a cup of coffee and some pastries. Toivo did a lot of translating and that is how we learned that the pastor was using many of my grandfather's sermons even though they were over seventy years old! He said also that they were written in excellent Estonian language. It made me feel good hearing that, and proud as well. It was another direct connection to this country.

After many thank you's and goodbyes, we left and continued on to our next destination.

"Now we will visit Parnu, a city on the Gulf of Riga," Toivo explained, as he slammed the door shut and started his old Volga. "In olden times it too belonged to the Hanseatic League but it is known now for its healing mud baths. It is Estonia's summer resort as well, with a long sandy beach."

As we traveled on the highway, my thoughts went back to my grandfather's house. I wondered what route he had taken in the winter of 1918 trying to reach the German front on the islands of Muhu. A friendly neighboring pastor had warned him of the imminent danger of the whole family being shot by withdrawing Russian soldiers, and how he had helped them escape in the middle of the night. Now I knew where the escape began and in a few days I would learn where it ended, since we also had plans to visit that island and Saaremaa.

Coming back to reality I noticed that the scenery was still the same flat land we saw since leaving Tallinn. Extensive woodland consisting mostly of birch trees bordered the road. There was hardly a car on the highway. I was on the lookout for storks. Spring was late this year and they were just now returning from their warm winter stay in Africa. Many houses had a large wagon wheel or a simple platform on their roofs inviting storks to nest. They are the bearers of good luck, people say.

After we arrived in Parnu, Toivo went to visit a friend and we explored the city with a map in hand. Walking along the street we heard people calling, saw many parked cars, and sensed some sort of excitement in the air. Men and women were dressed in their Sunday best.

"What is that commotion down the street? Let's go and take a look," I said as I started to walk a bit faster. "They are carrying blue, black and white striped Estonian flags. It must be something important."

People carrying the flags entered the Elisabeth church. We followed the crowd into the church and I noticed on the portal that it was built in 1747. We took a pamphlet from a table and sat down in a pew. It was a short ceremony. We found out later, it was the 120-year anniversary of the Estonian flag and the benediction thereof. The festivities continued outside with a military parade marching down the main street. As the people reached a small square, the band started playing lively marches and well-known songs, judging by the public's participation. Estonians love to sing and every five years they stage a song festival. Choirs from many countries join in and hotels as well as rooms are sold out weeks and months before.

Crisscrossing the city for about two hours, we saw many beautiful old houses and a few churches. An abundance of lilac bushes were blooming and the strong fragrance permeated the air. We saw many stands with a variety of flowers around the city, something I also had noticed in Tallinn. Then we met Toivo at the agreed time and place and continued our trip.

The next destination was Pallo, a small village southeast of Parnu, just a few miles from the Latvian border. Toivo's longtime friends Ants and Leili, both in their mid sixties, lived there on a small farm. They all had attended the same university in Tartu and always stayed in touch. Now we were to spend the night at their over one-century old house.

We took a leisurely tour of the farm. The fields were leased out to another farmer and had just been plowed. Blackbirds busily picked the worms. We headed to the woods close to Ant's house. The ground was damp and the air heavy and humid. The tall trees did not permit much sunshine to reach the forest floor. Decaying wood, rotting leaves, ferns and moss covered the ground, producing a musty, earthy smell. It was a heaven for all the little creatures living in dark places rich in humus. Only here and there a bird chirped. The silence made us whisper. Then, halfway down the path, in a small clearing, we were attacked by swarms of hungry mosquitoes and we hurried back to the house.

"The sauna is just about ready," Toivo said. "Ants started the fire yesterday so we can all enjoy it, and later we have dinner. You have to experience it," Toivo insisted pointing to me. "You were born in Tallinn and that makes you an Estonian by birth and all Estonians love it. It is part of our life."

During our walk they had pointed out a small house with an adjacent pond, and I had seen the smoke coming out of the chimney, but I didn't know what it was.

"You and Leili go first and we guys will take the second shift," Ants said pointing to us. "Leili then will have time to get dinner ready."

So, off we went.

It was a tiny log cabin. We entered a small room that served a dual purpose: a dressing room and also as a place to relax after the sauna. The telltale signs were the many beer bottles and glasses on the table in front of a couch and a pile of towels in one corner

We undressed and entered the sauna room. The heat and steam almost took my breath away. Leili, by way of sign language, had me lie down on an upper bench where it was even hotter and proceeded to strike my body with tender, flexible birch branches. It felt like sharp needles were pinching me all over, accentuating the heat. After she did the same to herself, she pointed to the door and had me follow her. Outside she quickly went to the adjacent pond, stark naked as we were, and waded into the cold water. I followed, slipping and sliding on the muddy lake bank, thankful for the darkness of night and surrounding bushes. Then the whole procedure was repeated once more. In retrospect it actually felt surprisingly good and I was very relaxed. That night I fell into a deep sleep, not waking up until morning.

After dinner we sat around the table talking, with Toivo translating. Old times were remembered and current events debated. It was then that we found out that Leile came from the same area in Kullamaa where my grandfather had lived and the place we just had visited. And to make it more amazing, my grandfather had married her parents. It had been his last official act as a pastor before returning to Germany in 1932.

The next morning we drove north to Tarvastu, my mother's birthplace. The house unfortunately burned down many years ago, but we took the opportunity to visit the nearby Mensenkampff's family private burial place up on a small hill. Weeds and grass were above knee height, making us walk in a single file. The chapel was intact but empty. The outside had been painted white and the roof replaced by a silver-colored metal one. The only tomb we could find was the one of my great-great-grandfather Carl von Mensenkampff who died October 4, 1878. It had a large cross, embedded on a pillar of stones and was easily visible.

I had just read about him in a book authored by his great-grandson Ernst von Mensenkampff and therefore knew a little about his life, his family, and his accomplishments. Now I also knew where he was laid to rest. I felt sorry not to live closer. It would have given me pleasure to tend to his grave and make it more presentable.

As we walked down the hill and crossed a fast-flowing creek, we saw the pastor in his black robe locking the church doors ready to go home. We caught up with him, explained who we were and he agreed to let us see the inside of the church.

It was a Lutheran church in the gothic style with a very high steeple. Hardly any paintings or other decorations adorned the walls. The one thing that caught my attention was a good-sized room in the back attached to the church on one side. In one corner was a four-to-five feet tall stove used to heat the room. A pulpit stood in the other corner, and the rest of the room was filled with pews for about 80-100 people. There were two doors, one to the outside and one leading into the church itself. This was the room where the pastor addressed the worshippers during the winter, when the big church was too cold. We could see neatly folded handmade afghans and colorful blankets on each seat for extra warmth and left there for use during the subsequent services.

Now I had seen another piece of the puzzle representing the country I had left as a young child.

"Our next stop will be Tartu, the intellectual and cultural center of Estonia and the second biggest city of about 100,000 souls as well." Toivo explained as we climbed into his old Volga. "We are very proud of the Tartu University. It was built in 1632 by the Swedish king Gustavus Adolphus and therefore is one of the oldest in Europe." He continued like the historian he was. "I also completed my studies here many years ago."

I had heard and read about this university. Many of my ancestors had studied there. They also had belonged to the local fraternity Livonia, were proud of it and many friendships emerged lasting a lifetime. It was very interesting for me to now see this university town along the river Emajogi.

"I think this is where you leave us, right?" I asked Toivo.

"Yes, I have to return home. Have some students who are about to take their final exams and I need to go over the material with them. You can take the bus from Tartu to Tallinn and then a cab to our house. I wrote our address on a piece of paper both in Estonian and Russian. You can't go wrong with that."

"Why do we need the Russian version also?

"Because most Russians here don't speak Estonian," Toivo replied shrugging his shoulders.

"But they have lived here for so long, 40 years and more!" I exclaimed in surprise.

Estonia was a free autonomous country for over 10 years now, but the distrust and resentment toward Russians was very much alive. People were very cautious dealing with them. I remembered an incident in Tallinn.

Toivo had hailed a taxi to take us back to his house. About one block before arriving, he directed the driver to halt the cab and we got out. Later I asked him for the reason of this and he answered, "I did not trust this Russian and I did not want him to know where I live." It was so sad to hear that. They were free and yet, they were not. Years of suffering and enduring the Russian regime for so long had left a permanent scar on their minds.

We drove through a few gentle rolling hills now, leaving the flat part of Estonia behind. Woods alternated with meadows and planted fields. It did not take long to reach the city limits and we didn't have any trouble finding the little hotel where we had made reservations. Lodging was cheap. We never paid more than forty dollars a night and that sometimes even included breakfast. Of course those places were not named "Four Seasons" or "Hilton", but they were clean and comfortable and that was all we needed.

After Toivo left and we had taken our small bag to our room, we headed to the old town of Tartu. To our surprise we were close to the university building, which was an impressive three-story structure. The center part protruded from the rest of the building, and had a gabled roof supported by six columns. As we continued walking we also discovered a statue of the founder of the university, the King of Sweden.

Criss-crossing the city for about two hours, I saw several points of interest to me because I had heard about them in my parent's conversations. The ruins of the Dom cathedral were impressive and showed what a large structure it must have been. They are a reminder of the times when Tartu was the residence of the Bishop.

As it was getting late we looked for a restaurant recommended to us for its uniqueness. It was an ex-gunpowder cellar built into an old stronghold moat dating back to the 18th century. Upon entering we were stunned. The ceiling was about 60 feet high. It had a main floor filled with tables and benches and along the sides above a galleria with more seating.

We had the typical herring with cream sauce and boiled potatoes. I love that dish and ordered it whenever I had a chance. Almost every restaurant had it on its menu.

The next day I wanted to go to the city archives. At the hotel they had given us the general direction but not the exact address. We had to ask somebody. We made several attempts, but nobody spoke English or German. We didn't even try Spanish.

"Let's ask these two nice looking ladies," I said to Alberto as I approached them. We were in luck. They didn't speak English but a little German and also knew were the archives were.

"Now see, I was right," I commented. "They looked intelligent and did you see how nice they were dressed? Very conservative and they wore a nice perfume."

Many older people in Estonia still have some knowledge of the German language. It was the most used language until 1887 when the official Russian language was imposed and made mandatory. The younger generation now is learning mostly English.

The archives were located in an old brown brick building adjacent to the park surrounding the ruins of the cathedral. Luckily the receptionist was fluent in English. We spent several hours there and walked out with a copy of my maternal great-great-great-grandfather's testament, and also a complete family tree showing him and all his descendants, as well as his parents and grandparents. Both documents were handwritten in the old German script not in use anymore. Luckily I was taught this writing in first and second grade and still remember some of it.

I was in heaven! I was so happy and excited! Until then I had more information about my paternal ancestors but now I finally found some from my Mother's side. I just wished we had more time to spend there. I was sure we could have discovered many more interesting things, but we had to catch the bus to Tallinn. Our stay in Tartu had come to an end. During the two and a half hour ride back to Tallinn we watched the scenery and were amazed of how many new expensive cars we saw on the road. Independence had done wonders for their economy.

The following day the sun was out and it was warm enough to wear short sleeves. We had made plans to visit the island Saaremaa this weekend, so Toivo's wife Evi, a college professor who was not retired yet, could join us on this outing. Evi was a very pleasant person, happy, and easy to get along with. She was almost as tall as Toivo and smart, teaching accounting and economics at the local university.

This time we took a bus. After about three hours we arrived in Virtsu where a ferry took the bus and us to Muhu. The ride on this large ferry, loaded with all types of vehicles, would last a little over an hour. We sat at a table for four along the railing and watched the activities below and then we cast-off.

"Here, have something to eat," Evi said after a while, as she handed each of us sandwiches wrapped in napkins and a cup of hot tea she had brought in a thermos. Busy with traveling and observing new sights, we did not realize how hungry we were. The home-baked dark bread with butter, a thick slice of cheese and ham was delicious and the aromatic tea was just what our stomach needed.

After eating I watched the vast expanse of the sea. No land in sight, just a few seagulls flying by. A slight breeze had come up. Some passengers had nodded off, slumped in their chairs. It was peaceful. And then the not so peaceful times came to my mind, the winter of 1918, the last year of WW I. My grandfather crossed this frozen sea on his friend's horse-drawn sleigh, in the darkness of night, far away from home, trying to reach safety with his wife and their five children. He had come to this same island we were approaching to find the stronghold of the advancing German soldiers. He must have been a courageous man with an enormous will to live and very protective of his family!

A slight jolt shook me out of my reveries. We had docked at the port Kuivastu on the island Muhu and passengers were hurrying to their respective vehicles to drive off the ferry.

We as well boarded our bus and departed toward the island Saaremaa. An about two mile long causeway built by the Russians took us from one island to the other. As we drove along the narrow highway to its main town Kuressaare, we saw a few windmills still working. They are the only ones left in Estonia.

After leaving our bags at a small Bed-and-Breakfast place, we crisscrossed the town and toured the Kuressaare Castle dating back to the 14th century. It had been the seat of Bishops and was situated within the Kuressaare Fortress surrounded by a moat. Then we visited the small and unpretentious Elizabeth Church dating back to the year 1240 and were surprised by how well preserved it was.

After a few hours of sight-seeing our stomachs demanded attention and our legs some rest. We took the advice of local people and had dinner in an old windmill made into a restaurant. It was good advice, the food was very tasty and the people friendly and helpful.

The following day we returned to Tallinn. Our wonderful vacation was coming to an end, but we wanted to see one more thing: the Kaarli Kirik, a large church in Tallinn where my great-grandfather Johannes Brasche was the pastor for 33 years until his death in 1906. To my disappointment the church was closed. The person at the church offices across the street was not able to let us in, but she showed us a portrait of my great-grandfather hanging in the vestibule. She also presented me with a book about the church. Unfortunately it is in Estonian, a difficult language I do not speak nor understand but it has a picture of my great-grandfather and his family. One of his sons was my grandfather.

From the church we went to the Estonian cemetery to find Johannes Brasche's grave. After searching for some time in the area indicated to us, I found the 105 year old weather-beaten granite headstone. The 12' x 12' plot was enclosed by a decorative but rusty metal fence. A few wildflowers were blooming and it was obvious, that somebody was clearing the area of major weeds.

I had found another root of my paternal family and it gave me a certain sense of belonging, of being part of this country I left so many years ago.

Now I had seen in person the places that before I had known only from conversations, as imaginary black and white pictures. Now I could relate to them closely having seen them in color, and I felt even more connected to this tiny country. I often wondered what would have happened had WW II not started, and had my parents and I remained in Estonia. My life would probably have been totally different. Nobody knows. As it is, I don't regret anything. I am happy where I am and don't want to change anything.

Tallinn

Alberto, Toivo, Evi and I having a good time.

My dad's birthplace in Kullamaa in 2004

Brasche's family plot next to my grandfather's church

Sauna and pond

Alberto, Toivo and Ants enjoying some happy tunes

Chapel and church

Carl von Mensenkampff (1808-1878)
My great-great-grandfather's grave

Lunch at a millstone table

The last windmills in Estonia

My great-grandfather's family
My grandfather is the first one from the left (seated)

My great-grandfather's church

Johann Heinrich Brasche's tomb stone in Tallinn
3-29-1843 - 5-24-1906
My great-grandfather

APPENDIX

ESTONIA

Estonia is a country in northeastern Europe on the Baltic Sea. It is the most northern of the three Baltic states. It covers 17,400 square miles, comparable to approximately twice the size of Vermont. In the west it borders the Baltic Sea, to the north is the Gulf of Finland, to the east Lake Peipus, and Latvia to the south. It has a population of about 1,400,000 people.

It is a largely rural country, flat in the north and with a few gentle hills in the south. The highest elevation is only about one thousand feet. Off the western coast lie many islands, the largest being Saaremaa and Hiiumaa.

The Estonian language closely resembles Finnish, and is spoken by about two-thirds of the present population of the country. The rest is Russian spoken by the many Russian immigrants and soldiers and their families who arrived during Soviet times. As Estonian is a Finno-Ugric language, it has no affinities with the language of the Scandinavian, Slavic, or the other Baltic countries.

Beginning in 1180 German merchants began to extend their travels to the east along the Baltic Sea establishing the trading cartel known as the Hanseatic League.

During the next 300 years many wars were fought between Denmark, Poland, Sweden and Russia. They all wanted the area that is now Estonia, Latvia, and Lithuania. In 1561 Sweden emerged as the controlling power. Estonia flourished under the Swedish rule. In 1632, Gustavus Adolphus, King of Sweden, founded a university in the city of Tartu, making it one of the oldest universities in Europe.

Sweden in time was unable to resist to the pressure from the east. Russia wanted a route to the Baltic Sea. Tsar Peter the Great conquered Estonia during the Northern War (1700-1721) and made it a province of the Russian Empire. He let the German Knights continue to act as intermediaries between him and the indigenous peasant masses, as had been done previously by the prevailing powers.

German Knights joined together to form three groups, one in each of the three Baltic provinces which are now known as Estonia, Latvia and Lithuania. The elected representatives ruled in an honorary capacity. Not to attend periodic meetings was considered a neglect of duty, a punishable offense, and had harsh consequences. Participating knights could not refuse a mandate and had to finance it out of their own pockets. For that reason only those knights were elected to the forum who had sufficient wealth to fulfill their obligations.

Beginning in the mid 1800s to 1918 people of German origin were called Baltic Germans to distinguish them from the Russians who began infiltrating the countries. Until 1914 they constituted about 7% of the population. Of these, 2% were the leading knighthoods as well as the pastors, all of whom lived mostly in the country. The other 5% composed of merchants and tradesmen were the prominent middle class in the cities with their guilds and brotherhoods. Many were highly educated and well traveled.

A big accomplishment of the baltic knights was the abolishment of the serfdom in 1842. The serfs now were allowed to buy and own land.

Estonians more and more became enchanted with the idea of becoming an independent country. University student fraternities created a blue, black and white banner, which eventually was to become the national flag. 1869 marked the beginning of a new tradition, the song festivals which united the people and remain active to this day.

In 1881 Tsar Alexander III ascended the throne. He was the first of the Russian Tsars not to marry a German princess. He was very anti-German and consequently did not ratify the agreements with the German knighthood which had existed for almost 170 years. An intense Russification began.

In 1888 Tsar Alexander III ordered everyone to speak Russian and forbade the use of the German language in public places, when in fact German had been the dominant language in Estonian academics, professional life and upper class society from the 13th century on. German schools had to close. All other schools in Estonia had to change over to the cyrillic alphabet, something nobody was familiar with. He imposed a ban on printed material in local languages and corporal punishment if students were caught speaking the local languages at school. To complete the Russification he installed Russian administrators and put them in charge of the region which affected the entire population in a very negative way.

In 1905 a liberal revolution broke out in Russia which spilled over to Estonia. Bolsheviks began killing landowners and pastors, for no reason other than having German ancestors. Manors and other buildings were set on fire by the hundreds. The country was ransacked.

Russian Kosaks were sent to establish some sort of order. Russification diminished and German schools were reopened although the new anti-german sentiment persisted.

At the end of World War I, encouraged by the fall of the Tsarist Empire, Estonia fought against the Red Army and the Landeswehr, a Baltic German militia who wanted to return to the old times. Estonians were helped in this battle by volunteers from Finland, Denmark, and Baltic German Freedom Fighters who supported the Estonian independence movement. On February 24, 1918, the Republic of Estonia was proclaimed. Soviet Russia finally recognized the independence of Estonia in 1920 by signing the Tartu Peace Treaty.

For twenty years Estonia was allowed to prosper as a nation. Then, in 1939 by a secret pact between the Soviet Union (Stalin) and Germany (Hitler) Estonia was again occupied by Russian troops and annexed forcibly into the Soviet Union. Part of this pact was that all people of Germans descent then living in Estonia and Latvia were given the chance to go back to Germany having to leave all their belongings behind. This had to be accomplished in a very short time. Some had only a matter of days to embark on German ships waiting in the harbor. All left. The alternative was the Gulag and/or death.

Russians flooded in. Tens of thousands of Estonians, opposed to the Russian regime, were deported to Siberia. About one hundred thousand Estonians fled to Western countries. The next fifty years were a hard trial for the remaining population. Resistance against Soviet control flared up periodically.

In 1989 Estonians, Latvians and Lithuanians joined hands and formed a 365-mile-long chain for the whole world to see their will to live in freedom. Two million people participated in this demonstration.

Finally came the day, when in August of 1991 Estonia declared the restoration of their independence. In 2004 they joined the European Union adopting the euro currency in January of 2011.

ESTONIA

PATERNAL ANCESTORS - BRASCHE

My early paternal ancestors were mostly Lutheran pastors, pharmacists or doctors. Later there were also a few teachers among the men, office workers, but only one pilot, my dad. Traditionally the oldest son followed his father's footsteps. Others left to work in larger cities like close by St.Petersburg, Russia. Many continued their studies in Germany, as there was always a close tie to that country. The German language was strictly maintained.

It is not known when and where the first man bearing the name "Brasche" lived and died. We do know that in the early 1200s many families with the surname Brasche or Brasch or even Braasch lived in the northern part of Germany, mainly in Mecklenburg.

Johann Brasch, the grandfather of the first Brasch(e) to live in Estonia, moved to the city of Lüneburg, in northern Germany, between 1730 and 1740. Where he came from and where he was born is not known. His date of death is listed in the church archives of that city as May 24, 1772. He was 78 years old.

Johann Brasch's son Johann Christoph, born August 22, 1739, became an agronomist and in 1760 moved to Prokent in the county Mecklenburg-Schwerin. Where and when he got married has not been established. It seems, though, that his wife's name was Dorothea Elisabeth according to church documents listing the birth of his first son Georg Wilhelm on October 12, 1760. His second child, a boy named Hinrich Franz Georg, was born May 2, 1762. Since Johann Christoph was new in the area, he chose the godfathers for his sons from the more prominent members of the community and named the babies after them.

Johann Christoph was a good agronomist and advanced quickly to become the manager of a small farm and later the right hand of a big land baron. Two more babies were born, Maria Amalia Henriette (Nov.10, 1765) and Maria Dorothea Elisabeth (Feb.28, 1770).

When Johann Christoph's second son Hinrich Franz Georg was sixteen years old, he made a contract with a local pharmacist that allowed his son to be a trainee in his pharmacy for six years. The chemist was to provide room and board and the boy's father all other necessities. The boy was not allowed to have any money, and any gifts he received he had to deposit with his teacher until completion of his training. At the end of the six years the pharmacist had to find him a job. The original of this "trainee contract" has been handed down through generations and was then deposited in the state archives of Schwerin for safekeeping and for future generations to view.

Many of the Hanseatic towns of Germany were in constant communication with the Baltic countries as trade flourished. The highly respected Burchart Pharmacy, founded in 1422, on Raekoja plats in Tallinn, the capital of Estonia, was well known among pharmacists in cities along the Baltic Sea. When the news circulated that the pharmacy was looking for a learned assistant pharmacist, 25-year-old Hinrich Franz Georg applied immediately. He obtained a passport from the mayor of the City of Lübeck, which is dated October 1, 1787, and reads something like this:

We, Mayor and Council of the free city of Lübeck, of the Imperial and Holy Roman Empire, announce and attest the fact that, thanks be given to God, the air in Lübeck is clean and healthy and no sicknesses among people and animals are noticeable. Hinrich Franz Georg Brasch(e) is of a mind to travel by ship to Tallinn and, to better his chances of success, desired from Us a certified note.

So executed in Lübeck, October 1, 1787

Ex commisione Ampl. Senatus in fidem

N.H. Evers, secretary.

This document was also deposited in the state archives of Schwerin.

Hinrich Franz Georg hurried to obtain passage on one of the last ships to sail to Tallinn. It was autumn and soon the Bay of Tallinn would freeze over.

He worked at the pharmacy for six years. On February 10, 1794 he married Margarethe Caroline Siemon, the daughter of a goldsmith working for an English jewelry store. With his wife's dowry Hinrich Franz opened up his own store selling herbs and spices. He registered as a citizen of Tallinn, and became dad to his four children: three girls and one boy named Johann Heinrich.

When the opportunity presented itself, Hinrich Franz Georg took over the management of the pharmacy in Haapsalu, a small seaside town south of Tallinn. A few years later, upon the death of the owner, he was able to purchase the pharmacy. He became a successful businessman as well dealing in real estate even though he never became proficient in the Estonian language. In 1805 he took advantage of the healing powers of the mud in that area along the coast of the Baltic Sea by establishing a bathhouse with six tubs.

Five years later, in 1810, his wife died. Necessity made him look for someone to run the household and take care of the children, the youngest being eleven years old. Thus sixteen year old Dorothea Beata Birkenfeld, the daughter of an acquaintance, came to live with them. Over time Hinrich Franz took a liking to her and, not paying attention to the concerns expressed by family and friends, he married her three years later. Two more children followed, a boy and a girl.

Upon the request of the citizens of Paide to set up a second pharmacy in their city, Hinrich Franz Georg looked into that possibility. To his surprise the existing one was very badly run and in poor condition. So in 1819, realizing that this was a good opportunity, he established a second pharmacy in Paide, a small town in the central part of Estonia. His oldest son Johann Heinrich, born January 25, 1799, had just finished his studies in pharmacology in San Petersburg and was returning to help and take over the business of the newly acquired pharmacy.

When Hinrich Franz Georg realized that his second son Georg Wilhelm did not have the desire nor the will to finish his studies and follow his father's footsteps, he sold the pharmacy in Haapsalu but kept the bathhouse. His youngest daughter helped him manage it since her three older sisters had married and moved away.

On January 21, 1848, Hinrich Franz Brasche was laid to rest in the family cemetery in Haapsalu.

On May 1, 1822, Johann Heinrich had purchased the pharmacy in Paide from his father for 6,000 Rubles and married Auguste Helene Dorothea Noericke. They had 13 children, of which three did not survive infancy.

Father and son had other similarities: both liked to buy real estate in foreclosure to later sell with a profit, and both had a small summer cottage in the country with horses and carriages, where friends were always welcome even for extended visits. It is said that in one summer alone 400 chickens were consumed.

In those days, before trains, cars and telephones, travel was done by horse-drawn carriage. Families in the country welcomed visitors, and guest rooms were always available. If more space was needed there was always straw in the barn for the younger folks to sleep on.

Visitors brought news from the outside world, even some gossip and often presents of items only available in the cities. It brought excitement into an otherwise monotonous life. It was not unusual to have visitors stay for weeks. Unmarried "aunties" were a very appreciated commodity, because they helped out with the children, the running of the household or nursed sick relatives back to health. They stayed for months, or even years, and sometimes never left.

Rudolph, the oldest son of Johann Heinrich, took over the pharmacy in Paide upon his fathers strong insistence even though he much rather had studied theology.

After 24 years of married life Johann Heinrich and Auguste Helene divorced. Two years later, on December 21, 1848, Johann Heinrich married Leontine Ackermann and they produced 4 more children.

Johann Heinrich's 13th child, a boy named Johannes born March 17, 1843, was my great-grandfather. He became a pastor of the Lutheran Kaarli Kirik in Tallinn. On January 19, 1871, he married Anna Wilhelmine (Minna) Hoffmann and they were blessed with four children. Two weeks after the birth of the last baby, Minna had a heart attack and died. Johannes was grief stricken. His children needed a mother. It was not until two years later that he decided to marry Minna's sister Selma Emilie Hoffmann. Three more babies followed, one of them named Arvid Leopold, my grandfather.

Johannes was a hard worker. With the financial help of German barons, and influential friends in the Tallinn Municipality he was able to purchase land to build and open a childcare center for 125 small children of working parents. As the number of children grew, classrooms were added. Soon new buildings followed and thus the Small Children Care Society was born, more commonly known as the Brasche Schools.

Their curriculum consisted of learning the stories from the Bible, math, and German and Russian languages. Until 1887 the most used language was German, after that only Russian was allowed. Education was based on Christian principals, cleanliness and obedience. All children wore aprons, blue ones for boys and pink ones for girls. On holidays and pastor Brasche's birthday they wore all white aprons. The children were given two meals a day and they could get seconds and thirds. After lunch came the handicraft lessons. Each day began and ended with a song.

Christmas was a big event that brought the whole community together. Impoverished families and their children were presented with food and clothing. Consequently, his parish grew from 3000 to 35,000 souls.

In 1900 the Kaarli Kirik Congregation had used all the plots in the cemetery and they were asking the city authorities for new land to expand. The petition was approved and for 2400.- rubles Johannes had a house built for the caretaker of the new cemetery.

Not all was good and peaceful though. Estonians and Germans were Russian subjects, having been conquered by Tsar Peter the Great in 1721. At that time the Tsar agreed to let the Estonians and Germans continue to take care of their own business and government, with no interference from Russia. In 1881 Zar Alexander III did not ratify the agreement Peter de Great had with the Germans, and the Russification of that region began. In 1905 Russian agitators infiltrated Estonia. It produced a lot of unrest and ultimately a revolution. Bands of Russians looted and ransacked the countryside, burning everything in their way.

A year later, in 1906, just after Johannes had confirmed a group of young girls, he suffered a massive heart attack and died. His sudden death moved the congregation immensely and hundreds followed the coffin to the new Estonian cemetery.

Johannes' son Arvid, born January 9, 1878, my grandfather, also became a pastor. In 1902 he was entrusted with the parish of Kullamaa. That same year he married Alma Sellheim. They had 10 children of which four died in infancy and a 19-year-old son succumbed to blood poisoning during his obligatory one year Estonian military service. During the 1905 revolution, his church and surrounding buildings were spared but unrest continued, culminating with World War I (1914-1918).

In 1918, for the first time in its history, Estonia became an independent nation. This was ratified by Russia with the Treaty of Tartu in 1920. But the situation did not improve. Agitators continuously stirred up hatred toward citizens of German origin. About 90% of their land, inherited or purchased, was expropriated. The leftover ten percent was barely enough to subsist.

The worldwide financial crisis of the late 1920 also affected Estonia. Therefore, when in 1932 Arvid was offered a parish in Germany, he accepted. He took his three youngest children with him. The oldest daughter Brigitte, already married and with children, and my father Ulrich stayed behind.

In 1938 Arvid made a bicycle tour with his youngest daughter, 18-year-old Lia, when he collapsed and died instantly of a heart attack.

My great-grandfather Johannes Heinrich Brasche Pastor in Tallin

Alberto and Rhona next to his picture visiting his church in 2009

My paternal great-grandmother
Selma Hoffmann (12-16-1854 to 11-24-1934)
Married to Johannes Brasche (3-29-1843 to 5-24-1906)
Pastor in Tallinn, Estonia

My paternal grandfather
Arvid Leopold Brasche (1-21-1878 to 7-7-19380
Pastor in Kullamaa, Estonia
Married to Alma Sellheim (7-21-1880 to 1973)

My grandmother Alma Brasche
at 17 years of age and 45.

OSCAR WILHELM BRASCHE

My great-grandfather's oldest brother, Rudolph, had taken over the pharmacy in Paide. According to tradition, his oldest son, Victor, (born March 11, 1862), who had studied pharmacology in the city of Moscow, should have continued the business. He disappointed his father, though, by wanting to stay in the big city. Now Rudolph's hopes were with his second son, Oscar, (born February 11, 1865), who had finished his studies in Tartu and had gone to St.Petersburg to find a job as a chemist in a big established company.

Rudolph traveled immediately to St. Petersburg to persuade his son to come back to Paide. Reluctantly, Oscar agreed. On January 1, 1893, he signed a purchase agreement: 8,000 rubles for the pharmacy and 4,000 rubles for the adjacent house, both at 5% interest. He was now the fourth generation of the Brasche clan to be there. Having settled and acquired living quarters, he was now able to marry Helene Krylow on July 3, 1894.

Work at the pharmacy was not fulfilling. He needed a more challenging occupation. Soon the opportunity presented itself to get involved in the city government. In 1898 he joined the city council and four years later became the mayor of Paide, a position he held for 16 years. Traditionally the job of mayor also included the position of head of the local church.

Oscar loved his new duties. They were just what he needed. Organizing, eliminating apparent obstacles, and getting things done were his trademark.

Improvements were made on the church grounds, modifications inside the church, and trees planted along the road to the cemetery a mile away. Oscar appealed to all the Brasche's to donate the money needed for a new colored glass church window commemorating the almost 100-year existence of that family in Paide. In no time the money was collected and a south-facing window to the right of the altar was installed.

Between 1900 and 1912, Oscar was the editor of a bi-monthly local newspaper in three languages: German, Estonian and Russian. Two elementary schools for Estonian children were established. A museum was created. A train line connecting Paide with the existing main route between Viljandi and Tallinn opened the possibility for better communication and trade. Large areas of swampy city land were drained and could now be leased to farmers producing income to the city coffers. City hall moved from a simple wood building hidden on a side street to a stone structure on the town square. The hospital was remodeled and beautification projects throughout the city were started.

Having always been interested in the history of his family, he had begun to collect material early on, and made notations when talking to his father or other relatives. In 1911 he was able to stage a family reunion. Family members were scattered all over the country and many were living and working in neighboring Russia. Oscar wanted to bring the family together. At the first meeting, 36 heads of households came, making it a real success.

His political career culminated in 1912 when he was elected to represent the Estonian cities in the Russian Duma or parliament. As such, he was invited twice to St. Petersburg to the winter palace of Tsar Nicolai II, to whom he was introduced, had a conversation with, and where he also had the opportunity to kiss the Tsarina's hand.

In 1817 he witnessed the beginning of the Russian revolution when their leaders requested that the Duma take over and form a new government.

In 1918 the Bolsheviks shot Tsar Nicolai II, the Tsarina, and their five children. They began to infiltrate Estonia and daily arrests and abductions of private citizens, Germans and Estonians alike, followed.

WW I was about to end. German troops, who previously had driven the Russian enemy out of Estonia, and had been received with open arms by Germans and Estonians alike, were ordered to retreat to Germany. Now the Estonians had to free their territory of the Russian invaders. Male Germans, young and old, helped in that effort, and together they succeeded. That same year a new Estonian government was established and consequently Oscar was relieved of all his civic duties.

Oscar then decided to leave Estonia with his family and return to Germany.

Once established there, he requested the help of all the Brasche family members he could locate. He wanted as much information as possible. In 1940 he finished his manuscript and a little booklet was printed.

Thank you! Thank you! Thank you! For without his inquisitive mind, all the Brasche history would have been lost forever.

Oscar Wilhelm Brasche
(2-11-1865 to 8-31-1954)

MATERNAL ANCESTORS

The family Mensenkampff originally lived in northern Germany. Hermann Mensenkamp is mentioned in city documents in the town of Lemgo, situated about seventy miles south of Bremen. This town, founded in the 12th century, was a member of the Hanseatic League, a medieval trading association of the free cities in several northern European countries, such as the Netherlands, Germany, Denmark and Poland.

Hermann Mensenkamp is mentioned several times in city journals as well, once in 1574 as guarantor for Johann Rubyth, and then in 1586 as witness in a trial. They also show that between 1574 and 1579 he received on several occasions two taler (old German currency) from Kaland, a religious foundation for his son's education. It is an assumption that Hermann was born in 1515 and died after 1586.

His son Jodocus or Justus in 1592 was registered as a student of theology in close-by Helmstedt, and subsequently ordained on March 2, 1600. Upon the orders of the abbot of the Corvey monastery in Heyen, he became a Lutheran pastor at a church in Heyen which is only about fifteen miles east of Lemgo. He died in Heyen in 1612.

Justus' son Henrich studied law in Helmstedt and in 1624 he became a citizen of Hameln where he opened his own law office. He married twice. Both of his wives were daughters of prominent families in Hameln. Of his eleven children many died as infants. Heinrich himself passed away in 1670.

So far the descendants of the Mensenkamp family had stayed close to Lemgo, but a son from Heinrich's second marriage named Justus Mensenkamp did otherwise.

He was born in 1628 and followed in his father's footsteps by studying law. It is not known where he went to school or when he left his hometown of Hameln and then Germany as well. It must have been after he graduated from Law school, since his name is not mentioned anymore. In 1655 and still in 1657 he was working as court secretary in Tuckum, not far from Riga, in the province of Kurland, which at that time was occupied by Sweden and now belongs to Latvia.

A few years later, in 1660, Justus' brother-in-law in Hameln received a letter from a friend living in the city of Mitau, Lithuania, in which he wrote him that Justus Mensenkamp resided in Latvia's capital Riga. He also told him that Justus had a fiancée and was about to be married. The future Mrs. Mensenkamp was Helena Reinken and her father was a judge for the autonomous Counts Oxenstierna. This family had immense landholdings and governed them like their own and separate country. The citizens of Wenden and Wolmar paid homage to them.

In 1664, through the marriage to Helena, Justus obtained a position with the counts of Oxenstierna. After working for them for eleven years he became chief assessor of the court of the diocese of Wenden. He probably worked there until his death in 1694, when he was on one of his many business trips to Stockholm, Sweden.

The peaceful reign of the Swedish king Gustavus Adolphus came to an end in 1701 with the start of the twenty-year-long Nordic war between Sweden and the Russian Tzar Peter the Great. It was a gruesome war. Nothing was left standing in the Baltic countries. Everything was burned to the ground or otherwise destroyed.

The life of the first Justus Mensenkampff born in Livonia (1675) was influenced by the events of that war. As a young man he joined the Swedish army and advanced to the rank of captain. He was taken prisoner in 1701 by the Russians and sent to a prison in Siberia where he was held for seven years. After his release he joined the army of Tzar Peter the Great as an officer. In 1725 he was elevated into hereditary nobility by a promise of Catarina I and was given *in arrende* (lease) the castle Mojahn. Unfortunately he died in 1732 at the age of fifty seven without having received the actual document.

His son Johann Justus, born in 1718 on the estate Mojahn, joined the Russian army as a seventeen-year-old. His career lasted 47 years, and saw him advance from sergeant to brigadier general and commanding officer of the fortress Kisinsk. Along the way he petitioned the execution of the nobility document promised to his father so long ago. He also applied for compensation for the many years of sacrifice in foreign lands. In 1742 his wish was granted and he was given a hereditary lease of the royal estate Aidenhof, which greatly improved his financial situation. In 1774 he finally received the certificate of nobility from Catherine the Great with an apology saying that the promise from Catherine I had been unfortunately somewhat unclear.

Johann Justus had five sons, of which four became Russian officers, and their descendants were assimilated by the Russian Empire outside the Baltic region and their whereabouts are unknown. The fifth son Jacob Heinrich Justus, born in 1778, studied law and acted as chief court assessor. In 1818 he acquired a large estate named Koenigshof. Two years later he completed the purchase of Tarvastu, which became the family's homestead for the next four generations until expropriation in 1919. He died in 1825.

This Jacob Heinrich Justus was my great-great-great-grandfather.

His only child, a boy named Karl Justus, was born in 1808. In 1830 he obtained his Law degree in Tartu, Estonia. With this certificate in hand, he served the province in diverse capacities in the court system, dealt with canon law, improved education and healthcare, and was elected representative of the people, including governor. But his talents were not only in public service, he had also an excellent business mind. He demonstrated this by acquiring four more estates.

He was becoming a wealthy and well respected man.

In 1832 he married Baroness Johanna von Kruedener and they had eight children, five girls and three boys, of which one boy died at the young age of thirteen. His two remaining sons followed the family tradition by studying law. Upon their father's death in 1878, the properties were divided among both. Jacob James, my great-grandfather, born in 1834 was entrusted with Tarvastu and two other estates. Ernst, born in 1840, received Puderkuell, Koenigshof, and two smaller land holdings.

Both brothers dedicated their lives to public service as did other large landowners. Most of them worked *ad honorem*, having their own private income from their personally owned properties. It was considered a duty and privilege to serve their native land. With good judgment and reason, Alexander the Great kept the Baltic territories under German guidance after the victory of the Nordic War.

As the years went by, political changes occurred. In 1880 Tzar Alexander III did not ratify the German knighthood and aristocracy. The Russian influence became more and more notorious. Latvians and Estonias, better educated now, began taking over the higher and critically important government posts. Therefore both brothers, Jacob James and Ernst, became agronomists and dedicated themselves to overseeing their properties.

Jacob James (1834-1913) lived in Tarvastu and in 1869 married Gabriele von Lieven. They had five daughters add one son named Karl August, my grandfather.

Karl August von Mensenkampff (1870-1939) studied agronomy in Estonia and Germany. After taking over the management of the estate and the landholdings in 1908, he dedicated himself to modernizing the farm equipment, imported breeding bulls from Denmark, installed generators that supplied electricity to all the buildings. He drained wetlands and improved ways to bring his farm products to the city of Tartu. He built a small harbor with adjacent warehouses at the river's edge and acquired a couple of barges to transport his harvests to the connecting railroad. He improved the distillery since alcohol brought good profits.

He loved his land and worked hard to improve it. But he also looked past the necessities by building several fishponds for carp to implement more variety on the dinner table. He started a pheasant farm to supply future hunts. He bought thoroughbreds for my grandmother, who was a passionate rider. He also built four greenhouses for her where she grew her roses, grapes, apricots and orchids.

The few years of peace were replaced by the turmoil, political unrest and then insecurity of WWI. Marauders wandered around the countryside destroying and killing everything in their way. Attacks on civilians occurred daily. Hundreds of manor houses fell to arson. My grandfather managed to escape injury and imprisonment by staying underground. At the start of the Russian revolution in 1917, he joined an army of Baltic German volunteers to fight together with Estonians against the Bolsheviks.

In 1918 Estonia established herself as an autonomous republic and reprisals against Estonians of German descent continued. My grandfather's beloved home Tarvastu was confiscated, leaving him only a small parcel of land and a house. His family and his mother-in-law moved to Dresden, Germany, for security reasons. His oldest son Curt finished his high school studies and followed the family to Germany to study engineering. Otto, the youngest son, remained with his father in Estonia but died two years later of meningitis.

Karl v. Mensenkampff's new business venture with a partner was unsuccessful and the partnership was dissolved after a few years. In 1937 his son Curt sent him a ticket for a transatlantic crossing with the invitation to visit him in Chile, South-America. They saw each other for the first time after seventeen years. He enjoyed his stay in Santiago and remained there several months. Upon his return to Estonia he worked as an accountant in the office of his brother-in-law Heinz von Ungern-Sternberg. On February 8, 1939, he died after a short illness at the age of 69 and was buried in Tarvastu, Estonia.

First page out of seven of Nobility document issued in 1774
by Catherine de Great of Russia

Fourth page showing the family crest
of the Mensenkampffs

Hand painted embellishments at the edges of the document

My great-great-grandfather
Carl Justus von Mensenkampff
September 23, 1808 to May 10, 1878

My great-grandfather
Jacob James von Mensenkampff
March 12, 1834 to October 30, 1913

My grandfather
Carl August von Mensenkampff
May 28, 1870 to February 8, 1939

Carl von Mensenkampff with son Otto

Otto Oswald Karl von Mensenkampff
July 16, 1903 to May 28, 1922

My Grandmother Mensenkampff
(4-17-1878 to 12-15-1934)

"Would you like to have this little notebook?" Aunt Dagmar asked me one day in 2003 when I was visiting her in Chile. "Your dad gave it to me when your mom died. I don't have any use for it but don't want to throw it away even though it is not very presentable."

"Yes, I would love to have it," I answered, as I reached for the small black booklet in her hand. The cover was worn, and some pages were loose. I could see it was falling apart.

Soon after returning from my trip I sat down with that slender little book in front of me. I was curious. Was it junk not worth keeping or had I received something interesting, a special find, something to be treasured forever? As I looked at it, I was full of excitement and eager to turn over the first page.

On the inside of the cover it said: For Mama from Karin. On the inside title page I read: Mama, Easter 1923. So it was written eighty years ago, a lifetime, and yet it had survived so many years. It had gone from Germany back to Estonia, then to Germany again. It even endured our escape from the Russians at the end of WWII. Then it crossed the Atlantic, sailed the Pacific and gone to Chile. Now it was in my hands in front of me. This surely meant that it was something important and very special to my mother, for nowhere did she leave it behind.

Turning to the next pages I saw my grandmother's very fine handwriting in the old German style called Sütterlin in use until the early forties. Having learned this for a couple of years in grammar school I could decipher it although, without much practice, some words were difficult and others I could not read at all. I immersed myself into translating the pages into the new German writing to make it easier to read and comprehend. What a wonderful story unfolded! It was the beginning of my grandmother's memoirs! It started like this:

When you my dear children were little and the nanny put you to bed at night, I waited for your calls, as I worked at my desk or read a book in the adjacent room.

I sat on your beds, one at a time, and we spoke of the sad and happy moments of the past few days. Finally you asked me to tell a story from the times I was a little girl, and then I talked and talked until your little eyes closed and you fell asleep. I wonder if you were dreaming of the healthy, dynamic girl your mother used to be. Yes, sleep well my dear children. May God look after you and give you the strength to conquer life and be triumphant. This was many years ago and now you asked me again to write my life story and so I will try my best to remember times past.

My home was an estate next to the ruins of a fort dating back to the thirteen's century built by the Knights of the Cross and which was later transformed into a castle. It was close to the city of Fellin (now known as Viljandi). Fellin was one of the nicest small cities in Livonia, with about 9000 inhabitants and home to a large German community. It had a very picturesque location on a cliff high above a lake. The view from our windows overlooking either the old ruins, or the lake below, or the extensive woods of the castle and surrounding fields was breathtaking.

I stopped and looked for the pictures I took of that place when we visited Estonia in 2004. We had walked among those ruins, which are now used for small outdoor theater presentations and songfests. My grandmother was right, the view is outstanding. Unfortunately, the house itself was gone. Now, about eighty years later, the city had doubled in size. Germans no longer lived there. A few older folks still remembered some of the German language they learned in school or had picked up by working with or for Germans. We had walked about this quaint old town, gone down to the lake and later visited an interesting museum. Reviewing the photographs I became more drawn to the story I was reading and wanted to know more.

In 1890, when Grandma was two years old, her family moved to a new place her grandfather had built for them just in walking distance from the old house. She describes the layout of all the rooms, of which there were many. It was a big house, a mansion. She refers to the paintings on the walls, which in time she all copied. I knew she had this talent. I have two of her oil paintings, as well as three small plates. They are the remnants of several sets of cups, saucers and bread and butter plates. She hand painted them all with different flowers in all colors. Her detailed work reveals her fondness of nature and the outdoors and she shows her father's love for it also.

The bare ground around the new house was soon transformed into a beautiful park. My father himself planted many saplings of noble firs in the grassy area in the front. He brought them from his father's estate and loved them dearly. Once Papa called me to his side and said: see child, soon these little trees will be as tall as I am. A few years later: look, now I have to use my walking stick to reach the tips. What wonderful elegant trees they have become. It is hard to believe that now they are around fifty years old. Are they still standing?..... Or did they become a victim of these very sad times, as everything else that one had cherished, loved and honored.

I stopped reading for a moment. The last sentence struck me deeply. Since this was written in 1923 or later in Germany she must have known about the loss of their land in 1919, when it was expropriated by the newly established Estonian government which had declared independence from Russia. Grandma really must have loved this country. I felt her longing for this place. She was homesick. Poor grandma! I felt so sorry for her.

The next day, right after breakfast, I continued reading. I could not help myself, I was intrigued and curious to find out more about my grandmother's life.

So far the words had not been too difficult to read. The penmanship was excellent, very small but neat and clear. Was this my grandmother's handwriting? The booklet had only one date: 1923. Grandma was about 45 years old then. Her eyesight had been failing for some time and she became practically blind in her forties after cataract surgery. Maybe she had written the first part and was now dictating to someone who, unfortunately, had a very bad handwriting and it was difficult to decipher.

From what I was reading I could tell that Grandma's childhood was a happy one. Dogs were her daily companions, horses became her love and riding in a buggy was her favorite pastime. Mademoiselle, a German lady who spoke to her in French, handled her with wisdom and knew how to direct her to some quiet activities as well. Grandma was home-schooled when the time came to learn the basics.

As a young teenager, besides playing the piano and painting, she showed other interest as well. She had a carpenter build a greenhouse for her where she grew grapes.

Social life was very active in summertime. Family and friends visited often, staying several days, even weeks, particularly when they came from far away. Cars did not exist. Travel was done with one's own horses or a stage coach. For Christmas the family alternated visits to the two sets of grandparents.

Her paternal ones lived nearby and could be reached in one day; whereas it required two days of travel to visit her maternal relatives. The first night they usually stopped at dear Uncle Heinrich von Wolff's estate. He was the stepson of her grandfather's brother. Grandma liked him and was always looking forward seeing him, and every time he had a little surprise for her.

I knew who this Uncle Heinrich was. His sister Isabella was married to count Ferdinand von Zeppelin. It took me a long time to find the Count's connection with my family. My great-great-grandfather's brother Woldemar married Isabella's widowed mother and thus became her stepfather. It was not a blood relationship with Ferdinand but interesting nevertheless.

I finished reading the last pages of Grandma's memoir and wished there was more, much more. I was thankful though that at least it had given me some insight into what her childhood had been. I knew now that she was a healthy and happy child, vivacious and energetic, enjoying her life and the love of her parents. Early on, she had piano lessons. She enjoyed playing. After she was married and had children, her son Kurt liked to sit under the baby grand piano and listen to her music.

She lived a simple life on their land where the food was mostly homegrown. A live-in seamstress made clothing for the whole family. Even fancy gowns emerged from her nimble hands. Rarely was something bought in stores. Most of Grandma's dowry was homemade as well.

It was fortunate for Grandma to have grown up during the last two decades of relative peace in the country, although dark and heavy clouds were already billowing on the horizon.

Grandma married my grandfather Karl von Mensenkampff on January 18, 1901. In the following three years she had two boys, Curt and Otto. In 1907 a girl named Rita followed. My mother Karin was her last child born in 1909.

For some time Grandma had felt ill with pain in her joints and legs. From what my Aunt Rita told me one time, it was now assumed, that she had muscular sclerosis, although in those days nobody had an explanation what was ailing her.

Every winter Grandma spent a couple of months in Germany and took healing baths to get relief and always returned feeling better and rejuvenated. Due to the political unrest in Russia, attacks by marauding Bolsheviks who ransacked the region, killing land owners and burning many manors, and the start of WWI, she did not want to leave her family and discontinued the treatments. Her condition became worse and she was forced to use crutches. A few years later, she was confined to a wheelchair. What was more painful to her than anything was the fact that she could not ride her beloved horses anymore. From early on riding had been the big passion in her life, a love she also passed on to her children, especially to Rita.

In the fall of 1918 it was decided that for security reasons she should leave for Germany together with her mother, her nine and eleven year old daughters and an Estonian maid. Her sons were to stay with their father. They got as far as Riga, Latvia. The German army was occupying the city at the time and it seemed peaceful. Her wishful thinking that the situation would improve made her decide to stay.

Suddenly, without much warning, German troops were ordered to retreat, which left the doors open for the Russians to occupy the city. There was no way out. Trains and ships were under Russian control. They were trapped. After several weeks of waiting and living in deplorable conditions due to shortage of food, Riga was liberated by an army of German and Latvian civilian volunteers. This gave the women a chance to continue on to Dresden.

Grandma's mother had bought a villa in a good neighborhood in Dresden and they were able to move in upon arrival. The girls were sent to school to give them a normal life with a chance to make new friends. Grandma depended on her mother's and her Estonian servant's help in all her activities. Friends from Estonia living in Dresden visited often, and tried to assist her as much as they could.

It was in 1920 when she was told that her son Curt was on his way to Germany to join her there to continue his studies. She was happily waiting for his arrival and fresh news from Estonia. She worried about all the loved ones she left behind.

All was well until 1922, when she received the devastating news that her son Otto had succumbed to meningitis in Estonia. He was only nineteen years old. She never got over this tragedy. Two years later another blow came her way. She discovered that her husband had an affair. They divorced. Now she was alone with three children. Not long after that, her mother began thinking of returning to Estonia. In time she sold the villa and Grandma had to find new living quarters for her family.

It now was the year 1927. The worldwide recession with high unemployment had began and her son Curt could not find a job. When told that in Chile were many opportunities for young professionals he took the chance. Saying goodbye to his mother was not as hard on him as it was on her. She knew she would never see or embrace her son again; whereas, he was excited about the prospect of finding work in far away lands.

His departure was the final blow. Grandma was tired, lonely, and homesick and a few months later she decided to return to Estonia. She longed to be with her family and friends and to live in her own home in familiar surroundings. To be away for nine years was just too long.

She settled in her house in Viljandi and her daughter Karin, my mother, took care of her now since her other daughter Rita had married and moved away. Grandma's health was slowly deteriorating. In 1928 she enjoyed the celebration of the arrival of her first grandchild, Rita's son Renaud. She lived long enough to get to know the young man who was courting her daughter Karin. They married in

1933. Grandma must have liked him. As a wedding present she gave him a Hirth motor for the airplane he was building. In June of 1934 she was able to hold her second grandchild in her arms, Karin's daughter, me. Then her health began to worsen rapidly and she died six months later on December 15, 1934, when she was only 56 years old.

I have copies of four pictures of my grandmother that are now over one hundred years old and most likely the only ones to exist. Looking at them I see the transformation from a chubby little girl in the arms of her mother to a young teenager with delicate features looking serious, almost sad. It was the way pictures were taken in those days. Nobody smiled, ever. I knew though that she was a happy child. Her grandmother called her her "pleasure bug". The other pictures show her as an adult, well dressed with short wavy hair, sophisticated, wearing a large frilly hat. I imagine her to be an intelligent well-educated woman, good mannered and proficient in painting and playing the piano. She also loved riding her horses, knew how to take care of them, and loved competition. She was an all-around lady with many talents.

I wish I had known her in person.

My great-grandmother Emily von Ungern-Sternberg (8-20-1855 to 12-3-19340)
and her daughter, my grandmother, Alexandrine but called Alice
(4-17-1878 to 12-15-1934)

My grandmother

My grandmother

My uncle Curt von Mensenkampff
(1-11-1902 – 5-14-2001)

It was January 11, 1912, Curt's tenth birthday. It was deep winter and fields were blanketed with a thick layer of snow. Trees struggled with the weight on their branches. All roofs had white caps. The air was freezing, but the boy's heart was warm and filled with anticipation. A big party was planned and he was allowed to invite all his friends, boys and girls, from his school in Viljandi. They had to be picked up with horse-drawn sleighs, and were now on their way to his home, Tarvastu. Friends and family were also invited to join the festivities.

Soon the sleighs would arrive. One could hear them from far away. The sound of the bells attached to the horse's harnesses carried far in the crisp air. A large covered porch led to the entrance of the house. Maids waited to help the guests peel out of their heavy fur blankets and winter coats and directed them to their rooms to freshen up. The drivers led the horses to the stable to keep them warm and fed.

Dinner would be served in the early evening followed by lively dancing in the big salon. Several pianists stood by to supply the music. For this special occasion, Curt wore a new black suit and felt very important.

Earlier in the day he had a birthday party on a smaller scale just with his parents and siblings. He was happy to see them all together and curious about what was to come.

"Son, come here," his father said with a smile on his face. "Your mother and I have a special surprise for you, now that you are older and more responsible." He lit a cigarette, prolonging the suspense, and continued. "Now, go and look in that old armoire." His younger brother Otto and his two sisters Rita and Karin watched excitedly as Curt walked over and opened the door. And there it was. His first very own rifle, a 6mm Bayard made in Belgium. Next to it was a box full of ammunition. He was ecstatic and thanked them over and over again. He could hardly wait for the next day to arrive. He wanted to go hunting with his friends.

The boys shot mostly black birds because they were a nuisance, ate small rabbits and plugged young birds out of their nests.

The party was a big success. For the adults it had been a pleasant distraction from the daily life filled with problems, worries and political uncertainty. For a few hours they were back in the good old peaceful times, enjoying delicious food and music. The dark clouds on the political and economic horizon were forgotten.

Curt was happy also. He had winter vacation and could be at home. In late 1908, after two years of homeschooling, he had been sent to Viljandi to attend school there. He first stayed with his Aunt Jeanette, his dad's sister, later with his grandparents Ungern-Sternberg, and finally at the boarding house Adolfi. Teaching was done in German but they also had to learn Russian, Latin and French. The Estonian language he had learned automatically at home while playing with the children of the employees and workers.

WW1 started in 1914. About a year later, Curt's mother moved with the children to Viljandi, feeling more secure in the small town. His father stayed in Tarvastu to run the farm.

The first years brought much unrest. In 1916 the school was closed. Trying to finish his studies, Curt went to Riga, Latvia, together with his uncle Heinz, only two years his senior. That lasted only a few months then that school was closed also.

Back in Estonia the situation became dangerous. Russian revolutionaries were burning and destroying everything in sight. In the winter of 1917 Curt, now barely fifteen years old, was arrested and taken to the Viljandi courthouse, where he joined many more people of German descent, among them the director of his school and several teachers. His mother and grandmother also were arrested but were allowed to stay in their homes. At midnight a large group was put on a train and taken to a warehouse in Tallinn, where more men were joining them from other cities until there were about six hundred individuals.

It was a big roundup of citizens of German descent. Nobody knew what was going on and what their future was. They slept on straw, which was hard on the older people. Food was scarce. Family members and friends living in Tallinn provided them with as much food as they could. After five or six days they were taken to a railroad station to be transported to St.Petersburg and from there to inner Russia. A man in charge of this maneuver saw Curt and noticed his youth. He sent him to a communist office located nearby. They questioned him extensively and he was released.

Curt immediately went to his Aunt Evi's house in Tallinn and told her about his so very exciting adventure, never thinking about the danger he had been in. After a couple of days, having cleaned up and eaten large quantities of food, his aunt put him on a train to Viljandi. His family was very relieved to have him back unharmed.

A few months later the Russians began to retreat. The first German troupes arrived in Viljandi and were received with much fanfare by Germans and Estonians alike. His grandmother's house became the officers headquarter and Curt one of their interpreters. In no time, all of Estonia was occupied by German soldiers. It became peaceful, but it was a deceptive peace.

During this period an Estonian government was established and a small army recruited. When Bolsheviks again advanced from the northeast, all throughout Estonia German volunteers gathered in the bigger cities. The retreating German army helped by leaving much needed weapons behind. Curt was among the volunteers. He, as well as everybody else, was instructed in the handling of larger weapons and hand-grenades. The purpose was to defeat the Reds, but this time together with Estonian soldiers and Finnish volunteers.

Curt participated in this defense action for many months. At the beginning he was stationed close to the Russian border where most of the fighting was. Later he became a messenger on horseback for commanding officers and as such he was always on the go. He loved riding. He had been in the saddle most of his life: first on his pony he received when he was four years old, later on any horse available. On his twelfth birthday his present was a four-year-old thoroughbred stallion, too small and not suited for racing, but good enough for him. The mare he was riding now was well trained and calm. More importantly, noisy explosions or whistling bullets did not spook her.

A nasty wound on Curt's leg that did not want to heal and prevented him from riding brought an end to his short-lived military career. He was released from service and sent to a hospital in Tallinn. Once healed and recuperated, he went back to his home in Tarvastu to join his father, who also was recently discharged. Curt's mother, sisters and grandmother had left for Germany.

It was time to make some important decisions. His school in Viljandi had been expropriated. He was now seventeen years old. He had lost a lot of time, did not finish school and therefore could not pursue an academic career as he wanted.

Then an opportunity presented itself in Tallinn. The German high school offered a six month intensive course for all the boys who had missed school through no fault of their own. A passing grade would give them the needed diploma. He registered. After the successful completion of the course, he returned once more to Tarvastu.

"Son, I think we have to follow the plan we had laid out last time you were here," his dad said with a somber voice. "You should go to Germany and reunite with your mother and sisters."

"Papa, I really would love to stay here. I love this place. I was born here."

"I know, I know. But you don't have a future here anymore. All this land has been taken away from us. All I have left are a few acres and this small house. It's not enough to live off. And who knows when the university here will open up again. In Germany you can continue your studies immediately."

And so it was decided. This chapter of Curt's life would come to an end.

Curt relished the few weeks before his departure. He rode his horse around Tarvastu to take one more look at all that was dear to him, and what had been his home until now. He knew every corner of this property, which now no longer belonged to them. He thought of the early mornings he had gone hunting in the woods. He liked the stillness with his well trained hunting dog at his side. He had fished in he lake patiently holding the rod, waiting for a nibble at the bait, and hopefully the big one to bite. Canoe trips with his friends on the nearby river were vividly in his mind. There were countless life-long memories connected with this place.

Together with his father he visited the well-to-do Estonian farmers in the vicinity. One invited them to a big wedding that lasted two days. Many guests were present and all knew his father. They gave his dad three cheers and cursed the government for having taken away his land. They admired him for being so calm about having lost his life's work. One of them said that he would have gone to the next barn and hung himself.

And then came the dreaded moment, the day Curt, accompanied by his dad, took the train to Tallinn where he was to board a small steamship. It was bitter cold and both wore their heavy coats and kept their hands in their pockets. Their fur hats made them look taller than they already were.

Dad and son alike were nervous but tried not to show their emotions. How long would they be separated? And what would happen to his dad and his brother Curt wondered. These were unstable times, another uprising of revolutionary elements could occur at any moment. There were many questions on their minds but neither one spoke out. Curt's dad had been a distant father, always occupied with overseeing the farm and running the business. There was little closeness between the two, yet they loved each other. They embraced, shook hands and Curt walked up the plank to board the ship.

He stood on deck clutching the railing. Seawater sprayed into his face mixing with his tears as he watched the familiar silhouette of Tallinn fade away in the horizon. The church spire was the last to disappear, and then there were only the white-capped waves of the sea. Even the birds had vanished. He felt very alone. It took a while for his young adventurous spirit to take over and direct his thoughts to the future.

It was stormy and the sea rough. The small vessel bounced from one side to the other. Quickly passengers retreated to their cabins feeling the onset of seasickness. Only Curt and an older gentleman remained on deck watching the heavy seas. Then the smell of food drew them to the dining room.

Due to the bad weather the little steamship arrived in Stettin with some delay. Curt immediately continued on by train to Dresden. His grandmother had purchased a two-story villa in a nice part of town with enough room to accommodate them all on the lower level and the family of a friend on the upper.

"Hello, hello, here I am finally. It is good to see you, Mama," Curt exclaimed as he bent down to embrace his mother who was sitting in her wheelchair. "It has been such a long time. Papa and Otto send you their love. And look at Rita and Karin, how they have grown." Curt was excited to see his family again, and they received him with open arms. They had not seen each other in almost two years. His beloved mother greeted her firstborn with tears of joy. The long separations had been hard on her. Worries about the wellbeing of her family in Estonia had caused her many sleepless nights.

Curt did not show how shocked he was to see the deterioration of his mother's health. She was only forty-two years old but looked so frail sitting in her wheelchair. It did not help that she was dressed nicely in a dark blue skirt and long-sleeved white blouse with a lace collar, and had her wavy hair cut in the latest style. He found out that she now depended on her mother's help and also on the strong muscles of the young Estonian servant who had traveled with them to Germany. She could lift her when needed. Fortunately there was a large circle of Baltic Germans in town that provided social life and companionship for the family and specially his mother.

The next few days Curt felt like a reporter. He had to answer in detail the never-ending questions about Estonia, their family and friends still there, the political situation, and what the general opinion was about the future of this country. His sisters wanted to know the where-about of the many dogs, ponies and horses they left behind. Had they survived, and were they well taken care of?

Curt had to see now how he could continue his studies. Having little knowledge of physics and chemistry and not enough of higher math, he began to take lessons in these subjects from a student in his senior year at the university. It was hard work and not easy. Curt failed his first attempt to enter the university but succeeded on the second try.

His studies were going well, when in 1924 they were interrupted again. The Polish army was marching toward eastern Germany. The university was closed.

All students, including Curt, volunteered to defend their borders. Fortunately this Polish aggression did not last long. Their army retreated and the university reopened. For Curt it meant a semester lost.

In the meantime his grandmother had sold the villa and returned to Estonia. His mother was forced to rent an apartment for herself, her two teenaged daughters, Curt and her caretaker. She had a small savings account. Her father, before his death in 1907, had opened it in Germany in her name. It came handy now, but they had to be thrifty.

In 1926 Curt passed his final exams at the university and was now an accredited engineer. During his summer recess he had applied for an apprentice job with the railroads to obtain a certificate as conductor. He was accepted and now was shoveling coal into the red hot opening under the steam engine's boiler to keep the freight train rolling. He also had to clean and lubricate the engine. It was hard work and mostly at night. During the day the railroad tracks were reserved for passenger trains. He advanced quickly to conductor assistant and soon after took the test to become a conductor himself.

Curt now had an engineer's title and conductor certification but no job. Times were hard in Germany. It was the beginning of the worldwide depression. Six million German workers were looking for employment. Curt was considered a foreigner. He spoke German with a Baltic accent. It would be impossible for him to find work. Hard decisions had to be made. Finally the family came to the conclusion that he had to go abroad.

Among his mother's friend was a lady who, before WW1, had met someone from Chile. It was a lady of German descent living in Chile and who at that time had been visiting family and friends in Germany. Both ladies became friends. They exchanged letters for many years and were still in touch.

"Curt, I will talk to Mrs. von Gersdorf," his mother said one afternoon, after wheeling herself closer to him at the table. "Maybe she can find out through her friend if there is a possibility to find work in Chile. It can't hurt."

"That is a splendid idea, Mama. No other prospects have materialized so far. We might as well try something exotic," he answered with a smile. "I do appreciate your help, Mama." Curt took her hand and kissed it. He was now twenty-four years old, loved his mother dearly and did not want to be a burden to her.

A month or two later the anxiously awaited response letter arrived. Yes, do come. Chile needs young professionals, and it will not be a problem to find a job.

After many discussions it was decided that he should take the chance and travel to Chile, a country situated on the other side of the planet in a different hemisphere. A long strip of land squeezed in between the Pacific Ocean and the Andes Mountains. A place not many people had heard of before.

It was not an easy decision for his mother to let him go even though she had originated this idea. She just knew that she would not see her son again. Curt on the other hand was very excited about the prospect of this adventure into unknown lands where he did not even speak the language.

Preparations were made for this long voyage. A couple of suitcases were filled with his few belongings and the very costly passage on the steamship General Baquedano booked.

It was the year 1927 and another chapter of Curt's life was beginning.

Curt was at another crossroad in his life, when he boarded the ship in Hamburg. The engines had already started. He could feel the vibration under his feet, as he stood at the railing. The seawater bubbled around the edges of the General Baquedano. He watched the ship slowly separate from the dock and back out of its moorings. It turned and sailed along the many births of this big harbor, passed by the shipyards, and entered the open sea. It was a warm summer day and Curt could not get enough of the sights.

They passed through the English Channel and headed for the northwestern tip of Spain, crossed the Atlantic, stopped in Rio de Janeiro and ended up in Buenos Aires, Argentina. There, Curt immediately went to the rail road station to buy a ticket to Santiago de Chile.

"Oh no, señor, the mountains are snowed in," the man behind the window said. "No trains are running now. You will have to wait until the tracks are clear," he continued with a smile.

"And how long will that take?' Curt asked in disbelief.

"Quien sabe. (Who knows).'' He shrugged. "Come back in a few days.'' And with that he stepped away from the counter. Curt was speechless. He never imagined that something like this could happen. He forgot that now he was in another hemisphere. He had gone from summer to winter during his transatlantic crossing.

A week went by until he could start the long trip through the vast expanse of the pampa to get to Mendoza. There he changed over to a narrow-gauge train to cross the Andes Mountains and then back to a regular train for the last leg to Santiago. It was almost a forty-eight hour ordeal.

As per agreement, he contacted the son-in-law of the Chilean lady. He stayed with them for a couple of weeks and received an enormous amount of information about Chile, their way of living, customs, and, very important, what not to do.

As it was a priority for him to find a job and learn Spanish, he took a room in a boarding house in downtown Santiago. The very first night he slept there he felt the building tremble. This must not be a very well built house if it shakes like that when a streetcar goes by he wondered. The next day he found out that it was not that at all but that he had experienced his first small earthquake.

Within two weeks time he had found employment. His job was to make the calculations for refrigeration systems to be installed in butcher shops, dairy farms, and restaurants.

In these years heating systems were unknown. Never before had Curt been as cold as in Chile, even though he came from a northern snow-filled country. Rooms in old building had high ceilings and the only source of heat was fireplaces. Fortunately the Chilean winters last only three to four months. In later years, with new technology, life improved and Curt's work included, besides refrigeration, also heating and air conditioning.

During the following months he met many people. Among them was a young fellow named Rolf von Schroeders, who managed a large farm in the outskirts of Santiago for his rich polo-playing uncle. Coincidentally this young man also was from the Baltic countries and they became best friends. They spent week-ends together visiting neighbors on horse-back. They joined the Santiago Paperchase Riding Club, bought the traditional white riding pants, red jacket, and black cap and in their black boots they looked smashing.

In 1930 Curt met and married Hilda Ovalle (11-15-1903 - 7-9-1945). She was of a good family. Her father Felix Ovalle Vicuna had died, and her mother and a younger brother lost their lives in an earthquake. She was in charge now of her two small sisters aged seven and ten. With the help of ex President Arturo Alessandri, her father's good friend, she got a well paying job and could make ends meet. The four of them moved to an apartment and became a happy family.

Ever since he had left Germany, Curt had maintained correspondence with his mother. Her letters were the only contact he had with his family. Shortly after Christmas 1934 he received a letter from his father with the sad news that his mother had died. He was still mourning his mother when two months later his good friend and riding partner Rolf succumbed to typhoid fever. Curt never went to the Paperchase club again.

This one letter Curt had received from his father was the beginning of a very active correspondence. In 1937 Curt was told that from his mother he had inherited a house in Tartu, Estonia, and was asked what he wanted to do with it. He told his father to sell the property and use the proceeds for a trip to Europe and then to visit him in Chile. He did and stayed three months. That was the only time when father and son developed a closer relationship and actually became friends.

As a young boy, Curt had enjoyed the frequent musical evenings at his grandmother's house in Estonia. His parents noticed his interest in music and bought him a cello. A Russian lady in town gave him his first lessons. That started a life-long love for this instrument and chamber music in particular. Being occupied with his studies in Germany, Curt did not find much time to play his cello, but the few moments he had he enjoyed immensely. Music was his hobby and a very important part of his life.

When in the early thirties he met Friedrich Dunker, he found a man with the same musical interest. Together with a few other musicians they formed a group of enthusiasts who gathered every week to play. In time they gave many well received concerts and their audience grew from just family members and friends to hundreds more interested in music. With the success of that little group, they founded the first chamber music orchestra in Chile.

Life was good to Curt. He had changed his job for a much better paying one. They had built a house, sold it, and built a larger one. The city limits of Santiago expanded, and they moved again farther away from downtown and its congestion. Things were going well.

Then came the downturn.

His father died unexpectedly in 1939 just a short time after Curt had received his last letter. And that was not the end of it. A few years later in 1945 his wife Hilda lost her long battle with tuberculosis. Curt was alone.

WW II had ended and he was worried about his two sisters, the only family he had left. He didn't know where they were, or what had happened to them. His imagination ran wild thinking of the worst. When he received the first letter from them, he was overcome by joy. They were alive!

In the coming months many letters crossed the Atlantic. The political and economic situation in post WWII in Germany was not the best, and the future uncertain. Curt's suggestion was for both his sisters, Rita and Karin, and their families to join him in Chile. After weighing the pros and cons they agreed.

In 1949 he made reservations for my parent and me on the Reina del Pacifico and in early May we embarked on the long voyage to Chile. Some time later my aunt Rita and her husband also made the trip. After over twenty-two years the family was together again.

At the beginning we all lived together in his house which was big enough to accommodate us all. I remember the lively conversation among them, as Curt wanted to know, in detail, all that had happened from the last time they saw each other. They refreshed memories of their childhood in Estonia. They remembered relatives and friends. They talked about others who perished in the war or had disappeared somewhere in Siberia, never to surface again, and the few who were lucky to return. Curt also contributed by telling his sisters about his life in Chile and all the adventures he went through. It was never-ending until late in the evenings.

Just as Curt had helped us and my aunt, he also financed the passage of another Baltic family consisting of husband, wife, and their twenty-three year old daughter Dagmar. After a few months, we noticed a new spring in his steps, a recurring smile on his face, and a twinkle in his eyes that was not there before. One evening, as we all sat around the dinner table, including Dagmar and her parents, Curt tapped his wineglass, stood up and cleared his throat.

"Now that you are all here, I want to make an important announcement." He looked at each of us and said, "I have proposed marriage to Dagmar and she has accepted." He took her hand and kissed it. "The wedding will be as soon as possible, since we don't see any reason to wait."

We all applauded and lifted our wineglasses for a toast to the new couple. We were very happy for them. It was a good day.

On March 13, 1950, they were married, and in the next three years two girls and one boy made their family complete. These and the following years were the happiest of Curt's life, and with this young family he had no time to get old. In 1992, he, then ninety, visited us here in California. His energy was never ending. I took him and Dagmar on a four-day tour through Southern California staying in motels along the way. In the evenings, after Dagmar had gone to bed, we watched the Olympic Games on Television until midnight. His endurance was amazing.

He quit his job at ninety-seven after working for the same company for seventy years. He passed away two years later after a short illness.

May he rest in peace.

Curt von Mensenkampff and Hilda Ovalle Esquivel
November 15, 1931

Dagmar von Hoerschelmann and Curt von Mensenkampff
June 9, 1951

AUNT RITA VON SCHULMANN

"My calls to Chile do not go through. I tried several times and always get this recording saying *unable to connect*," I complained to Alberto. I was so frustrated. It was the year 1988 and the phone-system was not what it is today. Long distance lines were often busy and calls very expensive. One minute to Chile cost close to three dollars compared to only a few cents today. I tried again and finally reached an operator who informed me that the numbers had changed and that she would connect me now. Finally I heard a human voice and I was able to ask for my aunt.

"There is nobody here right now. They are all at the cemetery. Señora Rita died yesterday," a strange woman's voice answered matter-of-factly. "She was in the hospital for a week and passed away." I sat down and could not believe what I had heard. Aunt Rita was gone. How could that be? I had talked to her about three weeks ago and she was fine. I felt my insides starting to shake. I was stunned. I did not cry. I was in shock.

As I sat at the kitchen table, dumbfounded, memories started to flood my head. The summer months my mom and I enjoyed with her on a farm in East Prussia in the early 1940s, my school vacations I spent with her in southern Chile, her visits to Santiago, when she came to see us in Malloco, and her precious few letters. She did not like to write and so it meant a lot to me that she maintained a correspondence with me when I moved to California. It did not matter that it was sporadic. She was always happy to see me and I liked staying with her. It felt like home. she was like a second mother to me.

Alberto made me a cup of tea and sat next to me. He knew that I loved my Tante Rita, as I called her, even though he had never met her. He tried to console me but didn't know what to say. He took me into his arms and just held me and it felt good.

"What was the reason of her passing? Did the woman say anything?"Alberto asked.

"No, she just said that Aunt Rita had been in the hospital. I should have asked. I didn't think straight. I will write a letter to Dagmar, Uncle Curt's wife, and ask for the details."

Aunt Rita was Mom's older sister. They were only two years apart. Both spent their childhood in Estonia, where they survived WW I. From 1918 to 1927 they lived in Dresden, Germany, and then returned to Estonia. Aunt Rita was a vivacious young lady, always ready to ride horses and also to compete with friends. I remembered her as being slender with dark brown hair, which later in life she kept cut short. She looked more like her dad, as did her older brother Curt. She had an oval face, her lips were thin, and her nose narrow. She mostly wore riding garb or slacks at home. Skirts or dresses were for the city. She was personable, uncomplicated, and always straight to the point. She was a strong person with a great sense of humor. Her optimism helped her through the many bad situations she was dealt in her lifetime.

Aunt Rita studied medicine but gave it up after a year or so to get married to Karl von Fircks, with whom she had a little boy named Renaud. This marriage lasted only three years ending in divorce. Two years later in 1932 she got married for the second time, but sadly she was unlucky again. Her husband, Alf von Ungern-Sternberg died, after two years of married life at the young age of 29.

The husband I personally knew was her third one, Uncle Harry von Schulmann whom she married in 1936. My first recollection of meeting him with Aunt Rita was in East Prussia in the early forties, where he was administrating a large farm close to Kalisz in the southwestern part of what is now Poland.

From what I remember and from looking at old photos, I figure Mom and I probably spent two summers there. Dad was in the German Air Force stationed in Italy and North Africa where he was flying large transport planes, the Junker 52's. He came to visit us there once and brought me a small bike from Italy. It was my pride and joy and it was good to have, when inn 1945, we had to flee from the Russian invasion.

My memories from those summers are wonderful. In the late afternoons, when the adults had a cup of tea on the back terrace, my aunt let me ride horses under her watchful eyes. I sat on a blanket and went continuously around the large manicured lawn, but I did not care. Being on a horse's back, feeling the warmth and strength of its body made me want to go on forever.

On hot summer days we walked to a small pond for a refreshing swim. After we were done playing in the water, big Rex, a black and white Great Dane, got his bath. Aunt Rita was his disciplinarian and he obeyed her. On the way back he carried the bag with our towels. We took walks in the nearby woods and I loved to pick flowers in the garden. My favorites were long-stemmed columbines in pale shades of yellow, pink, blue and lavenders. Aunt Rita's vases were always filled with them. Sometimes I played with little Polish girls. We got along fine without knowing each other's language.

Most days there was a lively coming and going of various horse drawn carriages or riders in front of the house. Friends or neighbors stayed for lunch; others came to consult and talk business with my uncle. I remembered my cousin Renaud also being there during summer vacation. He was Tante Rita's son and six years older than I. He showed me how to shoot a BB gun. We were aiming at sparrows on the rooftop. After many misses I had a hit and was very proud. It did not occur to me that I just had injured or maybe even killed a bird. I was too intent on hitting my target.

Renaud was part of the Hitler Youth. All boys in Germany had to join in those days. In early 1945 he finished high school and was immediately drafted into the military. He was only seventeen years old. About two months before the war ended, he was sent to the Russian front. We never saw him again. Aunt Rita contacted the Red Cross over and over again for years, but to no avail. It must have been heartrending for her not knowing what had happened to her son, her only child.

In 1945 she and Uncle Harry fled from the advancing Russian army like everybody else. There was only one direction: west. I remembered her telling how they drove their horses hitched to a wagon simply across open fields. The roads were blocked by hundreds of all kinds of vehicles and the going was slow. They were surprised that the wagon did not suffer with this rough treatment and that the trunk containing their few possessions, as well as the fodder for the two horses, did not fall off. With great relief they reached the western zone later occupied by American troops.

I didn't see her again until 1949, when we visited her and Uncle Harry for a couple of days before leaving for South America. Approximately one year later they joined us in Chile. After twenty-four years, the three siblings were together again: Aunt Rita, my mom and Uncle Curt.

Uncle Harry found a job, they made friends among the many Germans living in Chile, and eventually learned Spanish. They had adjusted to the life in this new country. Aunt Rita had horses again to take care of and Uncle Harry ran a large farm. They were happy. Aunt Rita's knowledge of horses became well known. People valued her opinion when buying or selling an expensive animal, and she acted as judge in many tournaments.

In 1980 Uncle Harry died. He had diabetes, was doing well, and just went for regular checkups. On one of those days they were waiting in the doctor's office when he suddenly fainted. After coming to he said that he had a wonderful experience. He had seen his mother and some old friends in a beautiful sun-lit flower-filled garden. Then he fell over and was dead. Aunt Rita never got over this loss and now she had followed him to that beautiful sun-lit garden. They are both buried side-by-side in Osorno, Chile.

As I was sitting at the kitchen table thinking of all these events that happened so many years ago, I had lost track of time. It was getting late. The sun was setting. I turned on the light and drank the rest of my now cold tea. With a sigh and a heavy heart I went upstairs to my desk to write a letter to Dagmar.

My aunt Rita von Schulmann
(5-20-1907 to 10-11-1988)

Uncle Harry von Schulmann and aunt Rita jumping

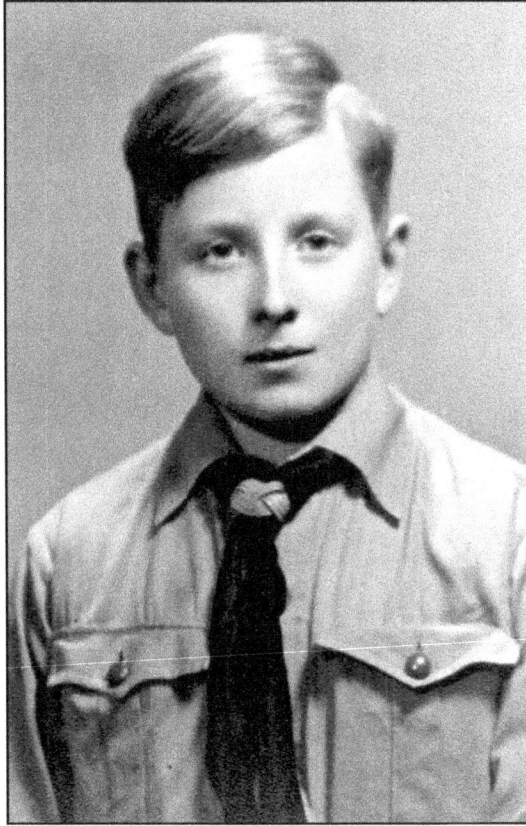

Last pictures of my cousin Renaud, aunt Rita's son
(9-28-1927 to 1-24-1945) MIA in WW2

Renaud and Rhona

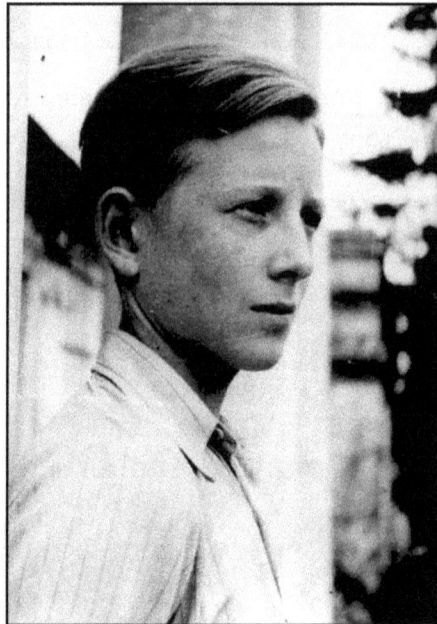

Mom, Rhona and aunt Rita at my birthday

My favorite passtime

Aunt Rita at 80 years old

ABOUT THE AUTHOR

Rhona Villanueva, was born 1934 in Tallinn, Estonia. Due to the political unrest in that country she moves with her parents to Germany before the begin of WWII. She lives in Berlin with her mother while her father is in the German Luftwaffe.

In 1949 the family emigrates to Santiago, Chile, where she finishes her studies, and finally in 1961 she changes hemispheres again and moves to Orange County, California where she now resides with her husband.

She writes this adventurous story for her children and their offsprings. She wants them to know how her life evolved, the ups and downs, the struggles having to learn Spanish and English, and to finally succeed.

www.ingramcontent.com/pod-product-compliance
Lightning Source LLC
Chambersburg PA
CBHW081509040426
42447CB00013B/3170

* 9 7 8 0 6 9 2 5 3 8 2 8 9 *